MOVING UP IN STYLE

MOVING UP IN STYLE

THE SUCCESSFUL MAN'S GUIDE TO IMPECCABLE TASTE

STEVEN WOODWARD NAIFEH AND
GREGORY WHITE SMITH

ST. MARTIN'S PRESS

For Carolyn and Linda

Manufactured in the United States of America

Library of Congress Cataloging in Publication Data

Naifeh, Steven W   1952-
    Moving up in style.

    1. Success. 2. Business etiquette.
I. Smith, Gregory White, joint author. II. Title.
HF5386.N32   650.1'4'024041   79-28528
ISBN 0-312-55070-7

Photo Credits

pps. 2, 52, 132, courtesy Saks Fifth Avenue.

pps. 12, 110, 184, courtesy Barney's Clothes, Inc.

p. 38, photo by Richard de Combray.

p. 66, photo by Ezra Stoller, Esto Photographics Inc.; courtesy Richard Meier & Associates.

p. 94, photo by Bettina Sulzer, courtesy André Emmerich Gallery, New York.

p. 156, courtesy Volvo of America Corporation.

p. 212, courtesy St. Maarten Tourist Office.

Acknowledgments

In the first chapter, we acknowledge our debt to the people who, in the absence of books and guidelines, taught us what we know about style. Several of these people also helped us in writing the book. Our thanks especially to Robert Ambrose, Harold Bernstein, James K. Chiu, Melissa Colbert, Samuel Dardick, Deborah Daw, Mark Dean, Alfredo Estrada, Bonnie Naifeh Hill, Stephen Hocschild, Hume A. Horan, Frederick Jemino, Richard Kvam, Arline Lanphear, Daryl Libow, Glenn David Lowry, Susan Lowry, Marilyn Machlowitz, Mary Ann Mannes, Alice Mroszczyk, Margaret Raines, Robert Rich, Catherine M. Soussloff, Stephen John Webster, and Madeline Wilson.

In addition, the proprietors or managers of these Cambridge and Boston establishments gave us advice in their respective fields of expertise: Alexander Bock of Bock Travel Service of Boston, Bruce Michael Friedman of Cave Atlantique, Scot Holman of The Greenery, D. Roger Howlett of Childs Gallery, John F. Horwath, Jr. of the Harvest Restaurant, Barbara Krakow of the Harcus Krakow Gallery, Stephen Patten of Wine For All Reasons, Bly Salzman of Music Systems Limited, and Susan Small of the Peacock Restaurant.

If it were not for the advice and encouragement of our close friend Richard de Combray, the book would not have been written. We want to thank Connie Clausen, our agent, for her crucial and unfailing support. Our thanks also to our attorney Martin Leaf, whose services we are particularly well-situated to appreciate. Much of the quality of the book is due to our editor at St. Martin's Press, the lovely Marcia Markland. John Crumpler, a friend at Harvard, helped us research parts of the book. Leslie Parsons performed heroically by typing an almost illegible manuscript.

Finally, we want to thank our families. They gave us ideas, encouragement, and, in the end, our fundamental belief that the most stylish life is a good life.

Contents

PART ONE:

Preliminaries

Chapter One:

Style

What Is Style?

We all wonder how others see us. Are they impressed? Are they critical? Worst of all, are they indifferent? Do we come across as intelligent, charming, and modest? Or slow, silly, and self-impressed? These are questions about *style*. Even if you never think about your style, the fact is, whether you like it or not, you have one. Even if you try hard not to act "stylish," that's a kind of style. This is the first important lesson about style: you can't avoid it. So you might as well stop for a moment and think about it. What kind of style do you have? Is it the right style for you? Is it the style you want?

Of course, to answer these questions, you really need to be able to see yourself as others see you. Few of us can get that kind of distance on ourselves. But most of us know how we would *like* other people to see us. Most American men today, it's fair to say, would like to be seen as attractive, knowledgeable, sophisticated, tasteful, self-confident, and, of course, masculine. In a single word, they want to have *style*. Not the overly refined British style, or the overly elegant French style, but the kind of rough, efficient, masculine style that has made American movie stars sex symbols around the world.

3

One thing is clear: Style is very important for success. Of course, talent, intelligence, and education are important too, but style is a key ingredient. Why? Because most people form opinions of you and make decisions that affect you on the basis of brief encounters. It takes time to find out how intelligent you really are, how well-prepared you are for the task at hand, or how persistent you are. But it takes almost no time at all to determine how stylish you are: how well-groomed, how knowledgeable, how well-mannered.

There are two ways to look at this. You can get very depressed about the fact that, at least on a certain level, superficial characteristics win out. Or else you can just accept the fact, and turn it to your advantage.

You can begin by learning the *rules* of style. The best way to learn them is by studying stylish people. There is a pattern to their lives, whether they're aware of it or not, and that pattern is *style*. Instead of just describing their lives and letting you figure out the pattern, we decided to reduce the pattern to a series of rules so it's simpler and clearer.

Of course, you shouldn't take the rules too seriously. After you've read them, try applying them to your own life, but only as you see fit. In the act of learning the rules, you can learn a lot about other things you've always wanted to know: how to look your best, how to enjoy the arts, how to make an impression. Learning to be stylish can be enjoyable, but it can also enrich your life.

The Ground Rules

First, the basics. Eventually we will get to a lot of specific recommendations on what to wear, what to buy, what to do, and even how to act. But first there are some principles that you should understand. They are the foundation for everything that follows. Read them carefully and turn back occasionally to reread them.

All Style Is Learned

Some people will tell you that good taste, good looks, and sophistication can't be learned. You either have them or you don't. This is not only arrogant, it's untrue.

How do stylish people develop their style in the first place? They weren't born with it; they learned it. They may have used parents or friends as models to learn from, instead of a book, but they did *learn* it.

In fact, taste and sophistication are no more innate than good looks. Of course, some people start with advantages—pleasant features, a good eye for colors, a fine disposition—but these are never enough by themselves. They have to be cultivated. Even the most "natural" style is the result of constant effort and years of practice. Practice, of course, is usually not a conscious thing. If you recognize that smiling a certain way seems to make people like you, you'll repeat it. Soon it will become a permanent feature of your personality. This process of adjusting to people's reactions never stops. And it shouldn't. You should just be more aware of how it works and how to control it.

There's No Easy Way to Acquire Style

Good taste, good looks, sophistication—each of these things takes a lot of work to develop. Things happen so quickly around us every day that we come to expect immediate results. If we don't get them, we are disappointed and lose interest. Diets. Crash courses. Exercise programs. If success isn't relatively quick and painless, we soon give up, or we never begin at all. Consider the bullworker, the strange stretching device that promises a muscular body in three easy weeks. Or speed-reading courses that promise to teach you how to read three or four times more quickly in the same short period, without losing any retention ability.

The major problem with these shortcuts is that they don't work. Any of them. Ever. Even if you get quick results, they don't last long.

How many people keep weight off that they've lost on a crash diet? How many people are really in shape after exercising for just three weeks?

Our puritanical notion is probably much more accurate. The only really good things in life take a lot of time and a lot of effort. Good taste, good looks, good manners, sophistication—in a word, style— are things you have to work at your entire life. But this shouldn't be depressing. Working at them doesn't have to be a form of drudgery. In fact, it can be highly enjoyable. There are a great many rewards in self-improvement. But before you can have fun at it, you have to understand that there are no shortcuts.

Avoid Artificial Things

Most of us think of style as artificial, as a face we put on for other people. But it isn't. Your style is you. When fully developed, it's as natural as your hair, your skin, your nose, or any other part of your body. After all, the only really stylish person is the natural person, even if that nature is acquired. The fact is that if you work hard enough at a skill, it eventually becomes natural. If you work hard at developing style, it will eventually be part of you.

So avoid artificial things. No artificial foods, artificial fibers, artificial gestures, artificial accents.

The corollary to this rule is avoid things that are beyond your reach. For example, stay within your budget. Don't buy cheap copies of the luxurious things that you can't afford. If you can't afford the leather and chrome Barcelona chair, don't buy an imitation leather and chrome version. Buy a fitted cloth chair from the Workbench or a similar store instead.

Another example: stay within your age range. Don't wear clothing that is too young or too old. Nothing looks less stylish than a mature man in jeans or a young man with a pocket handkerchief in his three-piece suit.

A final example: stay within your area of expertise. Don't claim to know something you don't. Don't feign an interest in a topic that really bores you simply because you think you *should* be interested. If you like jazz more than classical music or Agatha Christie more than Leo Tolstoy, don't counterfeit your preference; just consider changing it.

Avoid Excessive Materialism

In Colonial times, there were statutes called sumptuary laws that regulated clothing, eating, and other forms of "self-indulgence." If you were caught wearing a silk shirt or overeating, you could find yourself in jail.

But today excessive materialism seems almost a public virtue. After all, it's good for the economy. Yet the principal of Puritan behavior lives on. There's still something unseemly about living extravagantly. It means ignoring the problems and poverty of the world around you. That kind of boorishness is certainly unstylish and maybe even un-ethical.

What does this mean in practical terms? For one thing, it means you should avoid being ostentatious. There's an old saying that true wealth speaks only in whispers because it knows everybody is listening. The same is true of style. When you buy a car, for example, avoid buying the most expensive car you can find simply *because* it's the most expensive car you can find. The same applies to clothing. There's no reason to buy a $500 suit when you can buy a perfectly good one for $300 or even $200. Spending money just to spend it is always wasteful and almost always unstylish.

Less Is More

Half a century ago Mies van der Rohe, the great architect, framed his famous philosophy: Less is more. What he meant was that simple buildings without unnecessary ornaments actually look *better* than buildings with elaborate moldings and expensive decorations. In short, simpler is better.

Why is the simplest look usually the classic look? Because simplicity has the best chance of withstanding the test of time. That's why the simple dark blue wool suit is still the staple of every businessman's closet, why the simple cane-and-chrome dining room chair designed by Marcel Breuer in 1929 still looks good after fifty years, and why flowers are still the best gift for the woman you care about. These are the classics because they're elegant, and they're elegant because they're simple.

Simplicity is also a good rule for determining how you should act. Speak simply and clearly. Be honest and straightforward in your business and personal relationships. Maintain your dignity. Observe Thoreau's injunction to "Simplify, simplify . . ." In actions as well as in things, simplicity is the soul of true elegance.

Make Your Style Your Own

It's conceivable that an individual might follow all the suggestions we make in this book. But it's not likely. Very few people have the time or desire to develop a 40-inch chest, an in-depth knowledge of wine, a love of classical music, a perfect interviewing technique, and an art collection—all in the same life. Perhaps you're one of them. If not, remember that the idea is not to become adept in every way that a stylish man can be adept. The idea is to become adept in as many ways as possible.

You will probably find some chapters more useful than others. You may already have a 40-inch chest. You may decide you don't have the time or the will to develop one. On the other hand, you may want to learn about wines but just don't know where to begin. You may want to learn about clothing but may already know something about classical music. For others, the opposite may be true.

Everyone will come to this book with a personality and a set of interests that are unique. The very process of choosing to devote your attention to one chapter instead of another, the process of choosing the elements of style that are most appealing to you, will continue to make your style your own.

If you make your style your own, you won't need to worry about becoming a copy. Of course, there's nothing wrong with developing conventional tastes when those tastes are for the classics. Everything we recommend here is a classic. Everything from blue blazers to Breuer chairs has withstood the test of time.

This Book Is Only a Starting Point

This book isn't intended to set goals for you. We don't mean to suggest, for instance, that if you've bought all the records listed in Chapter Nine, you've mastered classical music. The various lists and explanations are intended to serve as tools for the beginner.

If you are a beginner, we suggest that you follow the recommendations carefully. But we hope that in following the recommendations you'll soon learn the principles they're based on. If you buy the wardrobe we recommend, for instance, by the time you complete it you should know enough about clothes to tell the difference between a good fabric and a bad one, a good color and a bad one, a good cut and a bad one. You won't need to consult our list—or any other list. Once you understand the rules, you have the right to break them.

It's like knowing good grammar. If you know what the rules of grammar are, and you have a good reason to break them—to express your thoughts more clearly, or to convey an idea that you can't convey in any other way—then you have the right to break the rules.

The same is true for style. It's only when you know why polyester is ugly that you can wear it properly. It's only when you know why red wine accompanies red meat that you can order a white with your veal. This book tells you what the rules are so that you can use them— or break them—creatively, constructively, stylishly.

PART TWO:

At The Mirror

CHAPTER TWO:

Clothing

Dressing in Style

Whenever you meet someone, the first thing they notice about you is your clothes. They can't tell how well-read you are or how much you know about classical music until a conversation begins, but they can tell immediately what you look like. Of course, your physical looks are important too. But most of us realize deep down that looks are not completely within our control. We can't really do much to change them. But we can change clothes. So we feel better about judging people by them.

First impressions are hard to forget. They linger long after you've had a chance to become better acquainted, long after you've found out whether someone is well-read or knows anything about classical music. And like it or not, first impressions are based on clothes. That makes clothes an important part, maybe the most important part, of style.

The Classic American Look

There are three basic reasons to care about your clothes: good clothes make you appealing to others, especially women; good clothes can help you in the business world; and good clothes are a joy to buy and wear.

From each of these standpoints, what we call the classic American look will probably do you much more good than the European equivalent. First, good honest materials and subtle coordination are more often found in the best American clothing than in European clothing. Remember, most women would prefer not to have too much competition in the way of bright colors and flashy materials from the men who escort them. A simple blue pinstripe suit is a much better foil for a wild gypsy outfit by Yves St. Laurent than men's clothes designed by Yves St. Laurent himself.

Second, it hardly needs to be pointed out that the classic American look in clothing is essential in the business world. It tells others that you're serious about your work, that you have taste but that you're willing to work within the conventions of Wall Street. Like it or not, a man who tries to interview for a job in a law firm wearing a rust-colored polyester suit with a floral tie is at a terrible disadvantage. The outfit may look snappy on the pages of a men's fashion magazine, but the lawyer interviewing him—who'll probably be wearing a gray flannel suit with a red polka dot tie himself—will look on the applicant as a stray from Mars.

Third, although classic American clothing may not be as flashy as European clothing, it's just as much fun to wear. As you'll soon see, it takes a lot of creativity and taste to put together the classic American look. You have to have a first-rate sense of color. You have to know how to put different textures together without having them clash. You have to worry about the exact fit of whatever you're wearing. Simplicity and harmony are hard to achieve.

Why the European Look Doesn't Work in America

Most books on men's clothing, like most magazines devoted to men's clothing, stress the European look. But the European look means tight fits, gaudy materials, and flashy combinations. It simply doesn't suit most American men.

Americans are built differently from Europeans. They are bigger and broader-shouldered. Although they are beginning to diet more and to worry more about being overweight, most of them would rather look well-built than slender. And the fact is that tight-fitting European clothes only look right on very slender men. A suit with an hour-glass waist is obviously wrong for a pear-shaped body. But it's also wrong for a football player's body.

European clothes look wrong on most American men for a still more important reason. It takes a certain attitude as well as a certain build to wear them. And men simply don't have that attitude in this country. In Italy, for example, men are often seen carrying handbags. No one there thinks much of it. But here in the United States, a handbag just wouldn't work. A snazzy European suit doesn't look quite as bad here as a handbag, but it definitely falls in the same category. So why risk it?

"Preppies" and the Classic American Look

The classic American look owes a lot to the stereotype of the "preppie." But—and this is very important—they are not the same thing.

A preppie typically wears bright green pants, a white button-down Oxford cloth shirt, a blue blazer, and, above all, Topsiders without socks. The clothes are expensive. But they aren't new, and they aren't too well-pressed. It's important to the preppie to have that slightly rumpled look.

This is *not* what you want to look like. Certain elements of the outfit are fine enough. In fact, the whole outfit is almost acceptable if you really *are* a preppie, if you're between fourteen and twenty-two and actually live on a campus. But no one should ever walk around city streets in bright green pants and no socks. In fact, no one should walk around a campus that way either, unless he makes a conscious decision that he *wants* to look like a stereotype. That's fine for those who want it. But the classic American look is far more subtle and varied.

Quality and Cost

How much money should you spend on a piece of clothing? Well, you have to spend a certain minimum amount to get good materials that are well-tailored. But this shouldn't worry you. How *many* clothes you own isn't as important as how *good* those clothes are. This is one place where the Europeans have the right idea. Instead of filling their closets with a lot of cheap clothes, they'll spend a fair amount on two or three really good outfits and wear them over and over again. This may seem boring at first. You may think people will wonder why you don't change your clothes very often. But if those clothes are classics, like any of the items we suggest, and if you take good care of them, all people will notice is that you're always dressed in good taste.

Even if you have to spend a certain minimum amount to get *good* clothes, you don't have to spend a fortune. There's no reason to buy them at a fancy clothing store with a vaguely European name. The walnut paneling, Oriental carpets, pirates' chests filled with strands of fake pearls, standing globes, and moose heads are theatrical props, expensive props that are paid for by the high cost of the clothes. Remember, you wear the suit, not the props.

So steer the middle course. You may be surprised to find that a good basic store like Barney's, Brooks Brothers, or Paul Stuart doesn't charge much more for a good suit than a less-established store charges for a bad one. There are also many stores around the country that sell perfectly acceptable copies of these clothes at substantially lower prices.

The Basic Wardrobe

We'll start with a basic wardrobe that every businessman should have. Most men already have a good start. If you own everything on the list, you ought to be well-dressed for just about any occasion. Even more important, if every piece of clothing you own appears on the list, and if you combine them the way we suggest, you can't go wrong. Because the suggested wardrobe is intended to serve as a basic list, there are no risky items. Everything has withstood the test of time. Details such as lengths of collars and widths of ties may change from time to time, but you should be able to wear most of these clothes today, next week, even a decade from now.

The Office

1. Three suits
    One dark blue pinstripe (all season)
    One plain gray (all season)
    One tan poplin
2. Seven dress shirts
    Three white
    Two light blue
    One maroon and white striped
    One blue and white striped
3. Six ties
    One blue and white polka dot (*a*)
    One red and white polka dot (*b*)
    One red and white striped (*c*)
    One red, white, and blue striped (*d*)
    One blue, white, and yellow striped (*e*)
    One red patterned (*f*)
4. Outerwear
    One raincoat with detachable liner

5. One light gray scarf
6. One pair black leather gloves
7. One black umbrella with plain wooden handle
8. One watch
9. One brown leather briefcase
10. One brown or black leather wallet
11. Two belts
    One brown leather
    One black leather
12. Two pairs shoes
    One pair black leather
    One pair dark brown leather
13. Nine pairs black knee-length socks
14. Nine pairs underwear
15. Nine T-shirts

After Work

1. One navy blue blazer
2. Three pairs pants
    One gray flannel
    One khaki chinos (all season)
    One khaki chinos (summer weight)
3. Two sweaters
    One light gray wool V-neck
    One dark blue wool V-neck

The Weekend

1. One down parka (chocolate brown, ivory, bright red, bright
    green, or bright blue)
2. Four shirts
    Three short-sleeve, long-tailed cotton (white, red, dark blue)
    One long-sleeve wool Pendleton (dark blue, white, and yellow)
3. One pair jeans

4. One tennis outfit (white shirt and shorts)
5. One bathing suit (black or blue nylon racer or maroon boxer)
6. One sweat suit (gray or dark blue)
7. Two pairs shoes
   One pair tennis shoes
   One pair running shoes

Night

1. Two pairs pajamas
   One short-sleeve (plain white or blue)
   One long-sleeve (thin gray, red, or blue stripes)
2. One pair brown leather slippers

The Ideal Wardrobe

We've started with a basic wardrobe. But most of us would like to have more than the basics. For those who want to expand their wardrobes beyond the basics, we've compiled an "ideal" wardrobe: a wardrobe as complete as anyone could ever want—or need. In fact, unless you're like Aristotle Onassis, who had twenty suits in each of his eleven homes, you probably can't use everything on the list. But it does give you some idea of what to work toward. It's also a good way to select additions to your current wardrobe.

The Office

1. Seven suits
   One plain dark blue (winter weight)
   One gray flannel pinstripe
   One dark blue pinstripe (all season)
   One plain gray (all season)
   One Glen plaid (all season)

One light blue seersucker
One tan poplin

2. Eleven dress shirts
   Four white
   Three light blue
   One light pink
   One light yellow
   One maroon and white striped
   One blue and white striped

3. Ten ties
   One blue and white polka dot (*a*)
   One red and white polka dot (*b*)
   One blue and silver striped (*c*)
   One red and white striped (*d*)
   One red, white, and blue striped (*e*)
   One green and red striped (*f*)
   One blue, white, and yellow striped (*g*)
   Two blue patterned (*h*)
   One red patterned (*i*)

4. Outerwear
   One raincoat with detachable liner
   One dark gray herringbone wool overcoat
   One tan or navy cashmere overcoat

5. Two scarves
   One light gray cashmere
   One red or blue and white polka dot silk

6. Gloves
   One pair brown leather for tan cashmere coat
   One pair black leather for gray herringbone and navy
   cashmere coat

7. Umbrellas
   One black with plain wooden handle
   One black folding traveling umbrella

8. One watch

9. One brown leather briefcase

10. One brown or black leather wallet
11. Two belts
   One brown leather
   One black leather
12. Two pairs shoes
   One pair black leather
   One pair dark brown leather
13. Twelve pairs black knee-length socks
14. Twelve pairs underwear
15. Twelve T-shirts

Of course, what you *wear* at the office will depend on what you do in the office—or on whether you work in an office at all. If you are a lawyer or a banker, three-piece suits in dark colors are essential. If you are an advertising executive, you can use your imagination a bit more.

The general principles are simple. The materials should be "honest." In other words, your suits should be *all* wool or *all* cotton. Polyester and other test-tube fabrics are not acceptable. "Textured" polyester—the stuff that's molded to look like real fabric—is particularly bad.

True, polyester fabrics don't crease. This has certain advantages if you have to pack your suits in suitcases a lot. You can take a polyester suit, wad it up into a ball, jump up and down on it, hang it back up on a hanger, and it will straighten out immediately. But how often does anyone have to wad a suit up into a ball and jump on it? Polyester is hot to wear, it's unpleasant to touch, and, more often than not, it's just plain ugly. It's not only "dishonest," it doesn't even hang right. Sure, it doesn't crease, but it doesn't bend either. What you see on the dummy in the store window is *exactly* what you'll wear home. There'll be no hint of a live body underneath.

You may think that all pinstripes look alike. They don't. There are stripes separated by a quarter of an inch and stripes separated by three quarters of an inch. Some stripes are distinct, others are chalky. Some stripes are bold, others are muted. The best stripes are fairly

close together, fairly distinct, and fairly muted. Otherwise, the suit
will remind you of Al Capone.

No matter how good the materials are, a suit can't look good unless
it's well-tailored. This means the basic design must be good. It also
means the suit must fit well. Unless you have a very unusual physique,
don't bother having suits tailored especially for you. Just make sure
the store you buy them at has a competent tailor to take in the seat
and make cuffs. If he has a foreign accent, you're in luck.

All suit pants should have cuffs of 1¾ inches. Harder to describe
is how the pants should hang. It's vital that they just barely touch the
shoes. If they are any longer, they won't hang properly. If they're any
shorter, they'll look as if you're trying to avoid puddles. Check your
sleeves, too. They have to be short enough to show a bit of the shirt
sleeve, but long enough to come to your wrists.

Some cautions to keep in mind:

Wear the right shoes when shopping. Most men buy their clothes
on Saturdays. If this is when you buy yours, be sure to wear the same
shoes you'll wear with the suit, not sneakers, since this will affect the
length of the pants.

Remember that few men are a perfect size. One arm may be longer
than the other. One shoulder may be higher than the other. Keep that
in mind whenever you are fitted for anything—pants, jackets, vests,
shirts. Be sure that the pant legs and sleeves match your legs and
your arms, not each other.

Don't be stampeded by the tailor. If the suit doesn't feel right when
you lift your arms or walk around, don't accept it until something is
changed.

Wear vests properly. Three-piece suits are essential for the business
world, but they look good whatever you do for a living. If you wear a
vest, leave the last button unbuttoned. The same holds for your suit
jacket too. (This arbitrary but universal style was set in England by
the Prince of Wales, later Edward VII, because he was too fat to
button the last button of his vest.)

Decide between two-button and three-button models. The basic rule is: If you're slender, choose the two-button style. It will show you off to best advantage. On the other hand, if you have a bit of excess tummy around the waist, three-button suits will cover it up much better.

Make sure you have your suits cleaned often. No matter how good a suit looks when you buy it, it will look terrible if it's stained or creased when you wear it. There's no reason to spend a lot of time and money acquiring good clothes and still look frumpy.

Don't forget about your shoes. There's a tendency to think that they don't really matter that much, since they're down there near the ground. Especially during the winter, it takes a lot of effort to keep them polished and looking good. But the effort is worth it. A good pair of shoes, well-polished, can make all the difference. By the same token a bad pair of shoes, or a good pair that simply looks sloppy, can ruin an otherwise stylish set of clothes.

The rule about honest materials applies to shirts, too. They should be cotton. All cotton. Cotton not only looks better, it feels more comfortable next to the skin. This means, of course, that your shirts must be laundered professionally. They should probably be starched as well. There's nothing more elegant than a fine white cotton shirt, perfectly clean and perfectly starched.

Although we are loath to concede the point, you can actually get away with a small polyester content in your shirts—no more than, say, 40 percent—especially if you're fairly active and want your shirts to look well-pressed throughout the day.

The width of collars is a problem. If a collar is too wide it will look flashy. If it's too narrow it will look stodgy. The best bet is to steer the middle course. Whether you wear button-down or loose collars is basically up to you. If you are wearing a three-piece suit, however, button-down collars are preferable since they won't keep creeping out over the vest. You should probably have some of both.

Some hints on shirt-buying:

Avoid shirts that are drastically tapered. This is important even if you have a tapered waist. A tapered shirt is too sporty for business attire, and one of the most important things about being well-dressed is knowing what suits the occasion.

Avoid short-sleeve shirts. Even during the summer, it's important to have part of your shirt cuff extend slightly beyond the sleeve of your suit jacket.

French cuffs are optional. But if you like cufflinks be sure they are simple. Very simple. Plain gold, silver, mother of pearl, or jade is best.

Ties should be silk, all silk. Avoid brocades; they resemble the interior of an overly appointed Cadillac. That's not the image anyone wants to convey. No knit ties, either; they're too casual. Also make sure that the designs are discreet. The polka dots and patterns shouldn't be too big. The stripes in the regimental ties shouldn't be too wide. Windsor knots are fuller and therefore better. When you've finished tying the knot, lift it slightly from the surface of the shirt.

For some reason, ties don't dry clean well. They lose their shape and color. If a tie gets too sloppy, the only real cure is to get a new one.

Avoid bow ties. Long ties look more serious, and they have the advantage of covering up your shirt buttons.

Even if you have a great suit, a great shirt, and a great tie, things can still go wrong. You still have to put the three together. Nothing is worse than colors that don't work together, except, possibly, the patchwork quilt dilemma—mixing patterns that just don't mix.

Some people think that the right color combination means wearing a blue suit with a blue shirt and a blue tie. Actually, this can be a disaster. Chances are good that the blues will clash or that there won't be enough contrast. Even the nicest colors can look drab if there's no contrast. Combine a blue suit with a white shirt and a red tie, for example.

Mixing patterns is equally difficult. Unless you know exactly what you're doing, you should never wear a striped shirt with a pinstripe suit. And if you wear a striped shirt with a striped tie, make sure the stripes don't compete. To help you decide what to wear with what, here's a list that shows all the ways that you can combine the suits, shirts, and ties we've recommended for your basic wardrobe. (Letters indicate ties listed in basic wardrobe on page 17.)

1.   Dark blue pinstripe suit
         White shirt, tie *a, b, c, d, e,* or *f*
         Light blue shirt, tie *a, b, c, d, e, f*
2.   Plain gray suit
         White shirt, tie *a, b, c, d, e, f*
         Light blue shirt, tie *a, b, c, d, e, f*
         Maroon and white striped shirt, tie *a, c, d, f*
         Blue and white striped shirt, tie *b, c, d, e, f*
3.   Tan poplin suit
         White shirt, tie *a, d, e*
         Light blue shirt, tie *a, d, e*
         Blue and white striped shirt, tie *a, d, e*

The raincoat must be tan. It can't be green or black. Whether or not it's a trench coat is up to you, but trench coats are usually better looking than the more conservative variety.

Jewelry isn't a good idea. Wedding rings are the major exception. You can also wear a college ring if you want to, although people should be able to tell that you went to college without consulting your hand. Anyone who does wear a college ring should make sure it's a simple gold or silver one with the college emblem on it, not one of those great ingots studded with a piece of colored glass.

Bracelets and necklaces are particularly bad. For some strange reason they are gaining popularity, but resist the fad. We hope there's no need to add earrings to the excluded class. Excess jewelry can only make someone look like a hippie, a madam, or Sammy Davis, Jr. The one exception is religious jewelry. A practicing Christian or Jew can get away with a cross or a star of David on a chain.

Selecting a watch is no easy matter. A watch doesn't just tell the time. It tells a lot about your taste. Keep it simple. (The Rolex Oyster Royal is the classic.) A stainless steel band is more suitable than gold.

And a simple white dial is essential. No pulsar watches; no jade, malachite, or lapis lazuli faces; no watches made from gold coins or the like. The same goes for high-fashion status watches like the Cartier tank watch which is a clear sign of trendiness. In fact, avoid any kind of watch that is *too* expensive. If you already own an expensive watch, don't get rid of it now. But if you are shopping for a new one, it is perfectly acceptable (in fact preferable) to buy one in the $50 to $150 range. A gaudy watch is just another piece of gaudy jewelry. It suggests that the owner is relying on his wealth rather than on his taste to establish his image. Pocket watches on chains are a feature out of novels and old movies and should stay there.

Tie bars and pocket handkerchiefs are also forbidden. They may be stylish, but they're just too fussy. You never want to look as if you spend too much time in front of the mirror each morning. Narcissism is never appealing in a man. Tie pins—simple ones, of course—are less unacceptable, but they should still be avoided unless you really feel uncomfortable walking around all day with a tie flapping about you.

Hats are another problem. Most men who worry about their appearance try to do without them. Most well-dressed men feel that a hat will mess up their hair, which is usually true, or that wearing one will make them look like characters out of a 1950s movie. It's no coincidence that American politicians would rather get frostbite than appear in a hat.

You should be *careful* about wearing a hat, but there's no need to do without one entirely. A tasteful hat, in either fur or felt, is acceptable. And it does have the advantage of keeping you warm. You shouldn't lose sight of the fact that clothing serves the additional purpose of protecting you from the elements.

Your shoes—*shoes,* that is, never boots—should be as plain as possible. They don't have to be tie shoes. But in any case, they mustn't be decorated with buckles, straps, tassles, or designer symbols of any type. The last are the worst. Needless to say, all shoes must be leather. Never wear brown shoes with a blue or gray suit.

A leather briefcase is more attractive than a plastic one. If you carry a briefcase, make sure that it's wide enough to be functional. A brief-case that's just wide enough to carry a folded newspaper makes the owner look as if he doesn't have enough important business to carry around with him, and he's better off not carrying one at all. It's all right to spend a fair amount of money on your briefcase. A handmade one can be very stylish, in the best sense of the word. Italian ones are usually the most attractive. But never exhibit any initials, either the designer's or your own. Initials make a briefcase look tacky instead of just stylish.

Like your briefcase, your wallet should be simple and made of leather. Black and brown are equally acceptable.

The socks you wear with a suit should all be knee-length. Save your legs for the beach.

Your underpants should be plain white boxer shorts or jockey-style briefs. There's a craze now for European-style underwear: sling-shot jockstraps or G-strings in hot pink. It's your body, not the shade of your underwear, that will excite your bed partner.

After Work

1.   Dinner jacket with accessories
       Shirt, suspenders, cummerbund, tie
2.   Four jackets
       One navy blue blazer
       One gray herringbone
       One plaid tweed
       One light brown cashmere
3.   Five pairs pants
       One gray flannel
       One khaki chinos (all season)
       One khaki chinos (summer weight)
       One gray corduroy
       One dark brown corduroy
4.   Ten sweaters
       Three cashmere V-neck (light gray, dark blue, fawn)

Four Shetland wool crew-neck (bright red, forest green, light
yellow, light blue)
Two cashmere turtleneck (beige, gray)
One natural-colored thick-knit Irish crew neck
5.   Three pairs shoes
One pair black patent leather
One pair oxblood Weejuns
One pair brown tie

A lot can go wrong with dinner jackets. Most of them look like
costumes for a musical comedy—pink, baby blue, and lime green
cloth piped with even brighter shades of silk. The shirts that go with
them look like dust ruffles on a chintz-covered bed. Avoid them. A
dinner jacket should be as simple as possible. All real elegance is
found in the cut and the fit.

Your dinner jacket must be black. The shirt and the suspenders
must be white—all white, solid white, no white-on-white. The tie
and the cummerbund must also be black—no crimson peeking from
underneath the jacket. At first an accent of color might seem to be a
good idea. But remember, a dinner jacket should be the most elegant
outfit in your wardrobe. And its elegance depends on simplicity. Keep
it classic: black and white.

The theme can be extended with a white silk scarf and a black
overcoat, although they aren't at all necessary. But keep away from
black capes and canes. Real elegance is never theatrical.

Your dinner jacket must be single-breasted. Notched collars are
more likely to outlast quick changes in fashion than shawl collars.
The shirt may have modest pleats, but certainly no ruffles. The cufflinks should also be simple, white gold or silver. Clip-on bow ties look
like clip-ons, so persevere and learn how to tie one yourself. Black
patent leather shoes are best, since they pick up the shine of the satin
facing of the pants, cummerbund, and jacket.

All four sports jackets must be 100 percent wool. It's hard to go
wrong with a blue blazer (no piping, of course), but be sure that the
buttons are plain. Sometimes a perfectly good jacket is ruined by

buttons decorated with anchors, eagles, or other gratuitous and objectionable motifs. If you like a jacket but it has buttons like these, simply ask the salesman to replace the buttons with simpler ones. On the other three jackets, you might try leather buttons (never imitation).

Double-breasted jackets look too European. They also come and go out of fashion quickly. Even when they are *in* fashion, which isn't often, they can only be worn by men who are very tall and very slender. You're better off sticking with single-breasted models.

The plaid jacket has to be chosen with special care. If the plaid's too bold, it will look like the one worn by the traveling salesman in *The Music Man*. A discreet mix of blue and brown is the most effective color combination, although it all depends on the material.

One place where most men's wardrobes fall down is pants. Men will spend lots of time and money on their shirts, their sweaters, or their coats and manage to do with a couple of pairs of pants that they rarely launder or dry clean. If you want to look stylish, your entire wardrobe must be of a consistent quality. Unlike suit pants, casual pants don't have to be cuffed. But cuffs are still advisable. Corduroy pants should be medium wale.

It may seem as if we've recommended too many sweaters, two for the basic wardrobe and ten for the ideal. But there's a reason for it. A sweater is a little like a tie. If you wear a different tie with the same suit, you've practically got a whole new outfit. Wear a different sweater with the same khaki or gray flannel slacks and you've practically got a whole new outfit too. The money you spend on sweaters, like the money you spend on ties, will buy a lot of variety.

The Weekend

1. Outerwear
    One light tan sheepskin jacket
    One down parka (chocolate brown, ivory, bright red, bright green, or bright blue)
    One tan or dark blue windbreaker

2.   Eleven shirts
      Six short-sleeve, long-tailed cotton shirts (white, pink, red, dark
         green, dark blue, and yellow)
      One short-sleeve cotton rugby shirt (white or dark blue)
      Two long-sleeve wool Pendleton (dark blue, white, and yellow
         plaid and plain maroon or dark blue)
      One light blue, long-sleeve work shirt
      One dark green, long-sleeve chamois
3.   Three pairs pants
      One pair white ducks
      Two pairs jeans
4.   One pair tan or dark blue short shorts
5.   One tennis outfit (white shirt and shorts)
6.   One bathing suit (black or blue nylon racer or maroon boxer)
7.   Running clothes
      One pair white or blue gym shorts
      One white running shirt
      One sweat suit (gray or dark blue)
8.   Two striped cloth belts (blue/tan and red/blue)
9.   Three pairs shoes
      One pair tennis shoes
      One pair running shoes
      One pair hiking boots

Jeans should be 100 percent cotton and straight-legged. Buy them preshrunken. Wash them frequently when you first buy them to fade and soften them. But beware: It's hard to look good in jeans. Because they should be worn tight, they show every contour of the body underneath.

The sweat suit should be all gray or all blue. No coordinated piping.

The same rule applies to the tennis outfit. It should be white—plain white. When a tennis outfit is decorated with colored bands, people wonder whether they're supposed to mean something. They don't, so they shouldn't be there. Since the only point of a sport is to move around quickly and easily, you need loose, cool clothes without frills. Save the color coordination for your other clothes.

Night

1. Four pairs pajamas
   One short-sleeve (thin gray, red, or blue stripes)
   One short-sleeve (plain white or blue)
   One long-sleeve (thin gray, red, or blue stripes)
   One long-sleeve (plain white or blue)
2. One bathrobe (white, green, brown, red, or blue terry cloth, or blue and white polka dot or blue and white striped silk)
3. One pair brown leather slippers

The pajamas are only indicated in case you wear them. It's in perfectly good taste to sleep in the nude. In fact, if you sleep with someone, it's probably in *better* taste. And it will certainly make you appreciate clean sheets.

The bathrobe should not be floor length and should not have a hood; if it is and it does, it's on its way to being a caftan. And that's not good.

Rules and Regulations

No matter what you buy from this list, you can't go wrong. But the list is far from complete; therefore we thought we should give you some of the rules we used in compiling the list, in addition to the general rules of style discussed in the introduction. There are only a few. But, armed with them, you should be able to venture beyond the list we've supplied and make your own stylish selections.

Don't Be Trendy

Fashion trends are dangerous. They pass quickly and you end up throwing away a piece of clothing long before it's worn out. The men's fashion industry does its best to change styles enough each year to make you buy new clothes before you need them. This makes sense for the fashion industry, but you shouldn't fall for the ploy. Clothes are expensive enough as it is.

But trendy clothing is bad for another reason. It shows that the wearer spends too much time thinking about how he's dressed. As we've pointed out again and again, even though all style is *acquired,* a truly stylish person should look unconcerned about his style, *as if* he had been born with it. No one who wears a tie that's too narrow, just because it happens to be the rage this year in a fashion magazine, looks unconcerned about his style. Never buy clothes that let people know *when* you bought them.

A perfect example of a trend to be avoided is the layered look— wearing as many clothes at one time as possible: two shirts, a sweater, a tie, two scarves, a pullover, a shawl, a jacket. A little of each layer is supposed to remain exposed so people *know* that you're wearing an entire wardrobe.

In fact, the layered look looks as silly as it sounds. But appearance has never distracted fad makers. Nor has practicality. The layered look is expensive to buy and hot to wear. Of course, if you've ever worn a sweater over your shirt, you've used the layered look to some extent. We don't discourage that kind of layering. But, as always, it should be subtle and restrained. Five or six layers of multicolored garments peeled back like the petals of a rose are neither.

No Designers' Logos

There's no reason to walk around wearing an advertisement for a designer who's already charged you too much for the clothes he makes. So avoid clothing with a designer's logo on it. Not just his initials—

Louis Vuitton luggage is the worst—but also keep away from anything with a designer's logo, such as the Gucci stirrups. Even the alligator on a Lacoste shirt falls victim to this rule. It's unfortunate, since some Lacoste shirts are among the best of their kind. But look for one without the ad.

Don't Wear Your Clothes Too Tight

Good clothes are never too tight. Of course, they shouldn't be too baggy either. The 1940s, when the baggy look was in, wasn't the height of men's fashion in this country. Your clothes should fit well. But not so well that people see your body before they see your clothes.

Suit Yourself

There's another set of rules to observe when you buy your clothes. The rules are related to you: where you live, what you do, how you're built. An outfit may look very chic on the pages of *The New York Times,* but wear it to the county fair in Pocatello, Idaho and you're asking for trouble. An important part of being well-dressed is knowing what is appropriate when and where.

Suit the Region

One of the advantages of the classic American look is that it's *American*—national, not regional. You can wear it in any part of the country: the beaches of California, the stately homes of Atlanta, the wintry byways of Wall Street. You can take a business trip to any corner of the country and wear whatever you wear at home.

Of course, there are *some* differences. Most of them have to do with weather. It's a matter of logic, not style, that you don't wear a winter wool suit on a warm day, even if that day happens to be in mid-January. So if you fly to Miami, take a summer suit. If you *live* in Miami, you may only need one winter suit (for those dreaded trips to Boston in January). Since it's warmer longer in Atlanta than in New York, you wear more summer suits in Atlanta.

You don't have to buy some kind of costume to suit the particular locale. White shoes look just as bad in Cleveland as they do in New York. An unconstructed jacket looks just as bad in New York as it does in Cleveland. You just see *more* of a bad thing in one place than in the other.

It's true, of course, that some parts of the country are more informal than others. A lawyer in San Francisco can wear a sports jacket to the office. His counterpart in Boston never could. So be aware of local custom. But don't be controlled by it. The fact remains, no matter where you go with the classic American look, you're *always* in style. A well-tailored, dark blue, three-piece wool suit will draw an appreciative nod no matter how casual the local customs.

Suit Your Body

If you're 5 feet 11 inches tall, weigh 150 pounds, have a 31-inch waist, and wear a size 40 regular, you'll look good in almost anything you put on.

Unfortunately, most men are one-of-a-kind sizes and shapes. If you belong to this vast majority, there are a few simple rules that can help you buy the clothes that will look best on *you*. For example, if you're tall, avoid pinstripes, especially pinstripes that are too close together. They'll only accentuate your height. If you're short, on the other hand, pin stripes can make you look taller. If you're overweight, avoid light or bright colors. They'll only make you look broader. Skinny people who don't want to look skinny should take note too.

We could carry this to a surprising level of detail. If you have short legs, don't wear cuffs. If you have broad shoulders, don't wear narrow lapels or narrow ties. If you have a long neck, don't wear flat, narrow, or unstarched collars. But the point we want to make is that the classic American look looks classic on everybody. Sure, there are tricks to make it look even better. But it will never look bad, no matter how idiosyncratic your body may be. That's one of the reasons it's a classic.

Suit the Occasion

In selecting the right clothes, *where* you live and *how* you are shaped are not the most important variables. The most important variable is what you *do*.

When you build your wardrobe, keep in mind how you spend your time. If you work in an office all day, every day, it's easy. You invest in suits. But if your work days are spent informally and you dress up only on occasion—a special date or a presentation for the Board— you may not need more than two or three suits.

When you choose what to wear from your wardrobe, you obviously want to think about where you're going. Just one little word of advice. It's always better to be a little overdressed than a little underdressed. And, of course, it's better to be a little anything than wildly out of place.

Breaking the Rules

Some rules should never be broken: Never wear a jumpsuit, for example.

Also:

No leisure suits.
No polyester.
No lavender.
No monograms on shirts.
No mirrored sunglasses.
No Hawaiian shirts.
No Army surplus.

No white leather shoes.
No Gucci shoes.
No Gucci anything.

But even if these rules should never be broken, most others can be—
under just the right circumstances.

Let's take an example. We've said that no one should ever wear
tight, flared jeans. The fact is, if you're young and fit, there are times
you can get away with it. The same is true even with European
clothing.

If there's a general rule, it's this: The younger, trimmer, and more
self-confident you are, the more rules you can break.

But this isn't always the case. There are some rules that mature
people can break that their juniors can't. A mature person can look
dignified wearing a pocket handkerchief and a tie bar. Someone much
younger will simply look pretentious.

If you don't feel self-confident about your own taste in clothing, or
you don't want to spend a lot of time thinking about the matter, use
the wardrobe we've provided. It's always safe. But our hope is that in
getting to know the list you'll also come to understand the principles
that underlie it. When this happens, you can begin to vary the wardrobe to suit your own style.

For More Information

John T. Molloy, *Dress for Success* (New York: Peter H. Wyden,
    1973).

Chapter Three:

Grooming

Grooming in Style

You may think good looks are important only for certain professions, acting and modeling, for example. In fact, looks are an important asset in almost all professions, from the most visible to the most obscure. When a political party selects a candidate, it wants someone who's intelligent, aggressive—and good-looking—someone who can compete with soap opera heroes for the attention of housewives. When a company picks a new executive, the best-looking candidate has an edge. For a salesman, good looks can mean more sales and quicker promotion.

Good looks also count after working hours. They can be an important factor in your social life, your emotional life, and, of course, your sex life. If you think women don't care how men look, think again. The old idea that the main aphrodisiacs for women were power, strength, wealth—something other than looks—was never completely true, and it certainly isn't today. Women do care, sometimes very much, how their men look.

The problem, you complain, is that good looks are like chicken pox. Either you have them or you don't. It's the luck of the genes.

39

Not so. Of course the Robert Redfords of the world do have an advantage. But even Redford works hard to be the sex symbol he is: He eats the right food, does the right exercise, and gets the right haircut.

So as you read, keep these two lessons in mind. <u>First</u>, <u>the way you look can seriously affect your life</u>. It can spell the difference between success and failure in the personal world as well as the working world. <u>Second</u>, <u>you *can* do something about</u> it. Good grooming may not be enough by itself. You also need the right clothes, the right exercise program, the right food, and a healthy dose of self-discipline. A $20 haircut is largely wasted if you don't get the vitamins your hair needs. But grooming is also essential to improving your looks. When the payoff is so great, how can you afford not to make the effort?

Keeping Clean

We assume that everyone who reads this book knows that the stylish man is, at the very least, a *clean* man.

We also assume that everyone knows more or less how to *keep* clean. After all, our mothers spent years telling us how to do it. And lest you forget the lessons now that mother is out of earshot, television repeats them every ten minutes or so. It hardly seems necessary to repeat them again here.

We wouldn't even bring up the point, except that most books on grooming and fitness published during the past few years devote hundreds of pages to the "art" of keeping clean. The level of detail is staggering. One book includes three pages on cleaning your fingernails. How does it fill three pages on the subject of nail cleaning? By informing the reader, among other items, to sand the edges of his fingernails, after he's cut them, with a fine-grain emery board used from underneath at a 30-degree angle. Who cares what angle you rub them at, as long as the end product is a well-groomed fingernail?

If anyone feels the need to be told how to take a shower or brush his teeth, we heartily recommend one of the following guides:

Charles Hix, *Looking Good* (New York: Hawthorn Books, 1976).
Henry Post, *The Ultimate Man* (Berkeley, California: Berkeley Publishing Corporation, 1978).
James Wagenvoord, ed., *The Man's Book* (New York: Avon Books, 1978).

Hair

The most important point about grooming is to get a good haircut. It's that simple. Simple, but expensive: To get a good haircut you need to go to a stylist. The neighborhood barber won't do. Stylists are expensive but well worth the investment.

If you're reluctant, look at it this way. If you go to a good stylist ten times in a year, it will probably cost you in the neighborhood of $150 for a year's worth of well-groomed hair. That's about the price of a summer suit. But you can only wear the suit twenty or thirty times before you put it away for the winter. Your hair is always on. Think of your hair as a piece of clothing that you wear every day, all year round, and you'll understand why it's worth the investment to go to a stylist.

What's the best style for you? The only way to find out is to ask someone who knows. Decide which of your friends has a good haircut and ask him for the name of his stylist. Then let the stylist tell you what he thinks will look best. After all, he's the expert, or should be.

One warning, however. Your hair shouldn't be *too* stylish, too carefully sculpted. You never want your hair to look as if you just had it cut, blow-dried, shaped, and shellacked with hair spray. Above all, you don't want your hairstyle to call attention to itself. As in clothing, all real elegance lies in simplicity. It's never flashy.

Also, avoid hairstyles that attempt to do what nature refuses to do. They violate the rule against artificial things. Remember, good grooming, like good clothes, should complement nature—show it off to its best advantage—not defy it.

Have you ever noticed men's hair in magazine layouts or in the movies? If so, you may have seen that few shots show every hair in place. Things have come a long way since the 1930s and 1940s, when men were *supposed* to look impossibly well-groomed. It's now acceptable, even preferable, to be natural. Remember this when you choose a hairstyle. Let it suit the way your hair naturally is. It will both look better and be easier to take care of. For example, if you have curly hair, stop trying to straighten it out each morning with a brush and a blow dryer. If your hair is well cut, you won't have to comb it at all. You can just step out of the shower, dry it, shape it a bit with your fingers, and be ready for the day.

The same rule applies for men with straight hair. Forget permanents, waves, and the rest of that rigamarole. Straight hair, well cut, is attractive and easy to take care of.

The length of your hair should depend on your hair and on your face. Here, again, your stylist should know best. But it also depends on your life style. Long hair (hair that covers the ears) isn't suitable for a career in business or one of the professions.

Dyeing Your Hair

Dyeing your hair is discouraged. For one thing, it takes too much effort. If you have it done professionally, it will add an hour to your stay and at least $20 to your bill. If you do it yourself, it takes more time, a little less money, and a lot more trouble.

But there's another, more important reason why we discourage hair dyeing. Unless you are graying at a very young age, it's *natural* to have some gray hair and *unnatural* to have jet-black hair. If your general appearance and your hair color don't match, people will notice, no matter how well-dyed your hair is. We are assuming you wouldn't try to change colors altogether, to become a blond, for example, even though you were born with dark brown hair. This *always* looks unnatural.

In any case, there's nothing unattractive about graying hair. It can look very good indeed. If you want to look young, it's a much better idea to stay in shape than to dye your hair. If you've got gray hair and good muscle tone you'll look comfortable with your age, *and* young in spirit. Don't fight aging. The battle will only leave you looking older.

If you want dyed hair to look natural (and that's certainly the next best thing to leaving it natural), you can't just dye it and leave it at that. It has to be dyed first, then dyed a second time with a closely-related shade. The process is called streaking. It will keep your hair from having the matte finish that's the dead giveaway of a dye job.

It's much too hard to streak your own hair. That's why we recommend you go to a hair stylist. He or she has better leverage, and a better perspective. Of course, it's expensive to have your hair professionally dyed, but if a man is vain enough to want to dye his hair, he should be willing to fork over the cash to do it right.

Hair Substitutes

The same principles apply to wigs, toupées, hair weaving, hair implants, hair transplants, and other artificial means of covering up baldness. None of them is ever completely convincing. The hair in a toupée doesn't move naturally. No matter what you do, a sudden gust of wind will always blow your cover. Remember, it's much more embarrassing to have people know you wear a toupée than to have them know you're losing your hair. Hair weaving and hair transplants are a little more lifelike, but a lot more expensive, a lot riskier, and a lot more painful. Just hearing what's involved will probably be enough to make you appreciate the virtues of baldness.

Hair Weaving. Hair attached to pieces of gauze is woven into the hair you have. The look is reasonably natural, but it only works if you've got some hair to begin with. As your own hair grows, the weave loosens, so it must be retightened periodically. Hair weaving makes it difficult to clean your scalp under the gauze, and it pulls at the hair you have, which actually accelerates the balding process.

Hair Implants. Matching hair—either natural or synthetic—is anchored to the scalp by surgical threads. The operation itself is painful and the stitches often become infected and reject the implanted hair. Even if the implants "take," they make shampooing difficult. Also, since any strain will break the stitches, active sports and other strenuous activities are forbidden.

Hair Transplants. In this process, hair is transplanted by the root from the parts of your head that have it to the parts that don't. The procedure is extremely bloody. A crust of dried scabs forms, then falls away within two weeks. The transplanted hair falls out too. But as long as the root remains alive, the hair will grow back. The success rate isn't good: Only 20 to 70 percent of the transplanted hairs survive the trip. If the transplant doesn't take, or if you lose the hair some time later, your bald head is left decorated with rows of scars that make a wig a necessity. Even if the hair stays put, the rest of your head will continue to lose its hair, leaving the transplanted hair in an unnatural patch along the places where you first lost your hair, usually around the temples. Again, a wig may eventually be needed to cover your bare crown.

So if you're losing your hair and can't adjust to it, go ahead and buy a wig or a toupée, the best one you can find. But you're much better off getting used to baldness. You may find solace in the fact that men like Yul Brynner and Telly Savalas have made careers as sex symbols out of their bald pates.

Facial Hair

Before you decide in favor of facial hair, you've got to ask yourself what it *means*. What does it say about you? Moustaches and beards are traditionally associated with a certain age group (older men) or a certain life style (outdoorsmen or academicians). Wear them and you're stuck with the association. Of course, if you *are* an outdoorsman—a park ranger, say—or an academician, and you want to look the part, don't hesitate to discard your razor. But if you're a salesman, an advertising executive, a government official, or a professional of any kind, you probably want to convey a very different image.

Regardless what you do for a living, however, the clean-shaven look is always preferable. It may only be a myth that moustaches and beards are dirty. Despite the considerable trouble involved, many men manage to keep their facial hair clean and well-trimmed. But it's a fact that a clean-shaven face looks "cleaner" than one with a moustache or a beard, no matter how carefully they're taken care of. Once again, it comes down to a question of how you want people to see you.

There is one kind of facial hair for which the rule is not flexible—sideburns. *Never* wear them long. As recently as the late sixties, long sideburns were somewhat fashionable. Men sported them an inch or two below the ear, sometimes letting them crawl onto their cheeks to form mutton chops. But today, fortunately, whatever fashionableness they once enjoyed has completely disappeared.

If you have very thick, soft facial hair the same color as the hair on your head, a moustache or beard *can* look good. Of course, like most things that are "difficult" to wear, they look best on men who are already good-looking. They can provide a finishing touch to a handsome face.

The other exception to the rule is that moustaches and beards can be useful in covering a bad feature: a receding chin, a long nose, an obvious overbite. If you feel insecure about one of these features and you've got the right kind of facial hair for a moustache or beard, we don't want to discourage you from growing one.

What about your eyebrows? Certainly we don't discourage *that* form of facial hair. But more and more often, men are joining women in plucking their eyebrows or having them plucked. There are two main reasons for doing so: first, to thin out eyebrows that are too bushy, and second, to separate eyebrows that run together across the bridge of the nose.

If you are self-conscious about your eyebrows for these or other reasons, don't worry about what the guys would think if they knew you plucked your eyebrows. When Communist Party boss Leonid Breshnev came to America several years ago, he had his brows plucked. His advisors told him that his thick brows made him look fearsome and sinister, an image he wanted to avoid on a diplomatic mission. No one accused him of being effeminate.

If you do decide to pluck your eyebrows, try to make sure they don't look as if they're plucked. Don't be too careful; don't shape them. As always, if you can't *be* natural, *look* natural.

One final word about hair. Whether it's on your face or on your head, whether it's yours or not, don't play with it. Insecure young boys have a nervous habit of playing with their own hair, running their hands through it, twirling it around their fingers, combing it incessantly. This habit can evolve into moustache twirling, beard tugging, and many other forms of fussing with facial hair. Don't do it. The relationship between you and your hair—or any part of your body— is for the bathroom and the bedroom. The only fingers that run through your hair should be someone else's.

Plastic Surgery

At one time only women considered having their noses changed or their faces lifted. Of course, that was when only women used hair spray. Even male movie stars had to sneak off to have plastic surgery done on the sly; it was considered unmanly. Today the situation has changed considerably. About 10 percent of all plastic surgery is performed on men and the percentage is growing rapidly.

You might expect from the rest of this book that we'd be against plastic surgery as the ultimate in defying nature. In most cases, we *are* against it. Frankly, we think you're better off learning to feel comfortable with your age and your appearance than going to the extremes of surgery to tighten your skin or alter your features.

Our society puts so much emphasis on youth and looking young that we tend to undervalue mature good looks or good looks that don't conform to conventional taste. Before you try to recapture your youth or transform yourself into someone you're not, you should at least consider the fact that a weathered face or a prominent feature can give you a *different kind* of good looks. Henry Fonda is as attractive today as he was at the age of twenty-five, but he's attractive in a different way. The media managed to turn Dustin Hoffman, Al Pacino, and John Travolta into major sex symbols even though none of them is conventionally handsome.

Yet artificiality is only one of the disadvantages of plastic surgery. Another is the cost. A complete face lift will run you about $5,000. Even a modest operation, such as a nose alteration, costs at least $1,000. Plastic surgery is also inconvenient. It involves one or two days in the hospital, then two or three weeks recuperating at home in a state of disarray that will scare away even your closest friends. Although the black and blue disappears within several weeks, the swelling will persist for as much as six months. To top it all off, the recuperation is painful. As with hair transplants, implants, and weaving, when you realize what's involved, you'll probably decide your nose doesn't look so bad after all.

Here are the major kinds of plastic surgery and what they involve:

1. The face lift (rhytidectomy).   The surgeon cuts a line from the temple to the bottom of the jaw, just in front of the ear. He pulls the skin tightly to get rid of the unwanted wrinkles around the mouth and jaws, removes the excess skin, and sews you back up.

2. Eyelid surgery (blepharoplasty).   The surgeon uses the same method to remove excess skin from around the eyes.

3. Ear surgery.   The surgeon makes your ears smaller by removing skin from the back of the ear and cartilage from underneath.

4. Chin surgery.   The surgeon either beefs up a weak chin by adding some bone, cartilage, or silicone or else modifies a heavy chin by removing bone or fat.

5. Nose surgery (rhinoplasty).   Again, the surgeon adds or removes cartilage to shorten or lengthen your nose, or to reshape it.

6. Skin surgery (dermabrasion, chemabrasion).   The surgeon removes scars, usually from acne, either by sanding your skin with a rotating wire brush or a steel burr or by applying chemicals that eat away the surface of the skin. In both cases, new, smoother skin forms.

As you can see, plastic surgery is no small matter. It's expensive, inconvenient, and painful. No one in his right mind would consider it lightly.

But there *are* times when plastic surgery might be a reasonable option. Some people are so upset by an unattractive feature, or by signs of age, that a look in the mirror can cause deep depression. If the depression lasts for more than a few moments, especially if it seriously undercuts a man's confidence in himself, the change might be worth all the hardships of plastic surgery. In cases like these, we recommend that you go ahead and investigate the possibility of having the appropriate operation. In general, we're against all self-improvement that smacks of artifice. On the other hand, we're strongly in favor of self-improvement that contributes to a man's self-confidence. You just have to weigh one against the other.

Makeup

The cosmetics industry has recently tried to tap what it calls the "large market" for men's makeup: men's rouge, men's eye liner, men's lipstick, and so on. The market should have remained untapped. Even bronzers—a form of rouge applied with a roll-on device and the most widely used of all the new inventions—are really just a cosmetic disguised with a masculine name. We recommend that you avoid bronzers, along with all other cosmetics for men.

Getting a Tan

A tan may help you look better, but it's hell on your skin. Moderate exposure to the sun can be good for certain kinds of skin conditions—especially acne. But prolonged exposure can seriously damage normal skin: The sun dries it out, ages it more rapidly, and sometimes even produces skin cancer. Suntan lotions can help protect you from these harmful effects, but only at the expense of your tan. No cancer, but no tan either. So do you have to stay out of the sun completely? Of course not. But you should think twice before spending every summer day and every available vacation looking for a sunny chaise lounge.

Your health is not the only thing you have to consider before stretching out for a tan. You also need to calculate exactly what the tan will do for your looks. Those of us who are concerned with tanning usually think that a warm tannish color is more attractive than pale white. But the esthetics are only part of the attraction. The rest is in what a tan *says* about a person.

Aristotle Onassis once said he kept a year-round tan for business reasons. Business associates would look at him and think that his affairs were in such good shape that he could make regular weekend trips to some sunny hideaway. That impression of wealth and leisurely confidence was a major asset in his business dealings.

But the fact is, very few people are in his financial bracket. If you keep a tan all winter long, your business associates won't assume you spend your weekends in the Caribbean; they'll assume you use a sun lamp. Your boss may think you never stay indoors long enough to get any work done. Your clients may assume that your play is more important than their business. Like any aspect of your appearance, a tan says something about you. Make sure it says what you want it to say.

Still, there's a time and a place for a tan. If the sun is shining outside and you don't overdo it, there's no reason why you shouldn't go ahead and sport a tan several months a year. You can even extend the tanning season a few weeks by using a sun lamp. Sun lamps don't give a natural tan by themselves, but they can prolong the life of a real tan. Even Onassis had to cheat every once in a while and use one.

Colognes

Never wear a cologne to the office. At work you want to smell clean, not sweet. You want to let your business associates know that you are serious and hard-working. A cologne will tell them just the opposite.

A cologne can be worn in the evening, especially when you're on the town, but don't use too much. You want the person you're with barely to *notice* the fragrance of your cologne. You want to hint at it, not hit her with it. A suggestion, not an harangue.

The problem is that you get used to a cologne as you apply it. You can apply too much without realizing that the smell is approaching combustible levels. Your companion will eventually get used to it too, but only after she's been overwhelmed by the first encounter, just when you want to create the best impression.

When you choose a cologne, just remember: nothing sweet or strong. Smell several brands and you'll soon establish a standard. Forget any nonsense you may have heard on television about one cologne's smelling more masculine than another. You can also safely ignore Joe Namath, Reggie Jackson, and the other sports superstars. Their sense of smell is for the millions they get for those ads, not for the cologne they're selling. You should also ignore price. Go for the smell, not the snob appeal. Very few people will recognize the name of the cologne anyway, or know how much you spent for it.

Once you've found a cologne you like, stick with it. Let the aroma of that cologne become a kind of signature smell that people will recognize as yours. Just make sure that it isn't recognizable from a distance. Your cologne, like your dress, like your style, should be subtle.

For More Information

Charles Hix, *Looking Good* (New York: Hawthorn Books, 1976).
Henry Post, *The Ultimate Man* (Berkeley, California: Berkeley Publishing Corporation, 1978).
James Wagenvoord, ed., *The Man's Book* (New York: Avon Books, 1978).

CHAPTER FOUR:

Fitness

Keeping Fit in Style

Fitness is a crucial element of style. The finest wardrobe and the most meticulous grooming are almost wasted if your body's not in shape.

We're not talking about endless exercise programs or crash diets. We don't think you should look like Arnold Schwarzenegger or like Mick Jagger. Your body is your body, and you shouldn't try to make it look like somebody else's.

Bulging biceps have recently become a national fad thanks to Schwarzenegger and Sylvester Stallone. But there's still something slightly ridiculous about them, and there's something definitely ridiculous about pumping iron all day long to develop them. Too much muscle—yes, there can be *too* much—is unsightly, it's a waste of time, and it's unhealthy.

On the other hand, if you have big bones, broad shoulders, or other generous features, that's fine. We don't think everyone should be thin or should try to be. In fact, the ideal American male has never been tall and svelte, like his counterpart across the Atlantic. He's usually average in height, broad-shouldered, and slightly stocky. His body hints at an athletic upbringing, probably in football. This is an ideal we can be proud to emulate.

What we should not be proud of is the fate of the *typical* American male. After they leave school or marry (whichever comes first), most American men allow their bodies to disintegrate. If you ever attended a high school or college reunion, you're probably familiar with the phenomenon: belts make a generous downward loop, pant seats hang low, shirt material lies loosely over the chest, faces seem fuller, fleshier. It's a sad sight and you don't want to have any part of it. You don't need to.

Staying fit isn't hard, and it doesn't have to be time-consuming. Yet it's the biggest favor you can do for yourself. You'll live longer, feel better, and look better for doing it. Nothing could be more intelligent, and intelligence is always stylish.

Staying Trim

Some points can't be stressed too much. Here's the first and most important one: stay trim.

How you do it doesn't matter. The best advice is simply not to eat as much. If you need to diet, eat even less than normal. How much less depends on your body size and your level of activity, but, for most of us, less means fewer than 1,000 calories a day. Reduce your calorie intake and you'll lose weight quickly and safely. Much more safely than with high-protein diets, grapefruit diets, and other fads. Eating less is not only a safer way to lose weight, it's also more permanent. Most people soon regain the weight they have lost on a fad diet because the diet doesn't teach them how to regulate their eating habits after they've gone off it. Counting calories and limiting your portions is crucial to staying trim *all* the time—whether you're on a diet or not.

The problem is, you have to watch what you eat not just when you have to lose weight, but every day. It's a lot easier and a lot healthier to keep constant watch than it is to ping-pong back and forth between overeating and crash dieting. If you learn to control what you eat all the time, eating properly will become automatic, like shaving or brushing your teeth. If you need reminders, you can step on the scale every morning. Another check is to keep your clothes fitting snugly. That way you can feel the first signs of unwanted weight.

Staying trim is a crucial part of keeping fit. Just remember the statistics: People who stay within their optimum weight range actually live longer than people who weigh too much.

Unfortunately, that argument doesn't seem to work for most of us (two-thirds of Americans are overweight). The penalty of death seems too far away—or else too inevitable—to worry about. Well, if the health angle doesn't convince you to stay trim, then do it to improve your looks.

Why do people look better when they're trim? For one thing, eliminating all that excess flesh allows your facial features to stand out. People see the features instead of just flesh. In addition, clothes must hang to look their best, and clothes can only hang on a lean body. Finally, people look more youthful, more athletic, and, let's face it, sexier when they're trim. Part of it is physical: Young, athletic, sexy people aren't flabby. But part of it is mental: People who are trim look as if they're in control of their bodies. People who are fat or even just fleshy look as if their bodies are in control of *them*. A trim body will make you *look* self-confident. That in turn will make you *feel* self-confident. And self-confidence is a key ingredient to style and good looks.

Nutrition

Despite the fact that our country consumes almost a third of the world's food supply, millions of Americans are malnourished. Don't misunderstand. When we say malnourished, we're not referring to those relatively few Americans who can't afford to buy the food they need. We're talking about the vast majority who *can* afford to buy the food they *don't* need. We're talking about you.

Doughnuts. Potato chips. Coca-Cola. Ice cream. Most Americans live on junk food. We're addicted to it. We consume $100 billion worth of it every year, and consumption is *growing*. The more junk food we eat, the less real food we eat. The bad crowds out the good, so we end up bloated and starving. Try to resist the temptation of junk food as much as you can and avoid this fate. Remember, *what* you eat is as important as *how much* you eat.

We're not advocating that everyone become a health food nut. People who talk constantly about their granola can be a little tiresome. Besides, an occasional ice cream cone won't kill you.

Our advice is simpler and easier. Just find out what foods you need to get a proper balance of protein, vitamins, and minerals, and make sure you get them every day. If you eat a balanced diet, you're probably already getting the amounts you need.

Another simple and relatively inexpensive way to make sure you get the right amounts of vitamins and minerals is to take a supplement pill. Protein is more difficult. You can get it in pill, liquid, or powder form, but you have to take a lot of pills, a lot of liquid, or a lot of powder to get enough. Unless you're trying to put on muscle, you're better off making sure that you eat a certain amount of protein-rich food each day: meat, fish, eggs, cheese, beans, or nuts. Get a copy of *The Brand Name Nutrition Counter* by Jean Carper (New York: Bantam, 1975). Find out how much protein there is in the foods you eat. Then ask yourself after each meal how much protein you've just consumed. If you don't think it was enough, make up for it at the next meal. Pretty soon, eating the right *kinds* of food, like eating the right *amounts*, will become a habit.

The best general book on nutrition—it's surprisingly scientific for such a readable book—is Adele Davis's bestseller, *Let's Eat Right to Keep Fit*, revised edition (New York: Harcourt Brace Jovanovich, 1970). Many of the book's diet recommendations are too specific and too demanding for most people to follow exactly. It would take a brave man to drink the pep-up brew that Ms. Davis herself drank every day of her life. But by the time you finish the book, you'll be convinced of how important a good diet is to your health and to your looks. The book concludes with a very complete chart that gives you the calorie count, as well as the protein, vitamin, and mineral values, of most foods. It's a valuable list. If you're interested (and you *should* be), read it and refer to it often.

Smoking

Don't.

Exercise

You can't change your looks. But you can and should make the most of what you've got. And one of the best ways to look your best is to exercise.

But exercise isn't just a cosmetic device. It's a crucial part of staying healthy. A good physique will not only make you look more attractive, it will help you live longer.

The sorry fact is that most men give up exercise the day they leave school. Even high school and college athletes often hang up their sweat suits and jockstraps the minute they settle down. Why? Because most popular school sports are *competitive* sports—baseball and football, for example—not *fitness* sports like swimming and running. Competitive sports usually require a lot of time, a lot of support, a lot of equipment, and a lot of other people. Therefore, the end of school (which provided all these things) usually spells the end of sports. The result is that many football players have turned to flab by their fifth reunion. But it doesn't have to be that way. What they need to do— what *you* need to do—is to find a form of exercise you enjoy enough to make it a lifetime pursuit, long after you've left the playing fields of high school and college.

But what *kind* of exercise?

It depends on what you want out of it. Some exercises are good for your lungs, some are good for your heart. Some exercises give you strength, some give you endurance. Some improve your muscle tone, some your muscle definition, some your flexibility. Figure out what you want or need from your exercise and choose it accordingly.

Some sports do everything. They improve everything except your speaking voice. They're good for your heart, your lungs, your strength, your flexibility, and your looks, to say nothing of your sexual stamina.

Endurance

At the core of any exercise program are the aerobic sports, sports that build endurance by exercising your lungs and cardiovascular system. The range of aerobic sports is very broad, and it doesn't matter which one you do. There's cycling, skiing, and jumping rope, in addition to the most popular ones—tennis, running, swimming, and squash. All that's important is that you *do* choose one of them, and that it makes you sweat—sweat hard.

Some aerobics are competitive sports; some are individual. If it's competition you like, try the court sports—tennis, squash, handball, or basketball. You can still play these when you're pushing ninety. They can even be played (in fact, they have been played) from wheelchairs.

You may have difficulty getting started. Courts and partners can be hard to find. But once you've found them, make a regular thing out of it. Many a lifelong friendship has been made on the court. Take advantage of the opportunities for *both* good exercise and social relaxation.

Table tennis is sweet and it allows you to converse and have a drink while competing, but unless you play at championship level, it's about as much exercise as holding the yarn while your wife knits. In short, it is *not* exercise.

The same is unfortunately true of mechanized golf. Mechanized golf is golf with a cart to carry you around. It may be a nice way to spend an afternoon outdoors with friends, but don't kid yourself into believing that it's exercise. And walking from hole to hole doesn't turn it into exercise. You'd have to walk a dozen miles just to burn off that sandwich you ate in the clubhouse. Even carrying your bag around with you (considered *very* athletic among golfers) requires only the slightest exertion.

Don't misunderstand. Golf is an admirable pastime. So is chess. So is stamp-collecting. But it's not exercise. It will do very little for your health, and the only thing it will do for your looks that chess won't is give you a tan (and only on your face and forearms at that).

But maybe you don't have the money to rent a squash court. Maybe you don't have the time to find a partner. Maybe you don't like competitive sports. Don't despair. There are many sports you can enjoy on your own. Swimming and running are the best examples. Of the two, swimming is better for you. It exercises your arms as well as your legs and lungs. On the other hand, running is easier—and you don't need a pool.

To really improve your health and appearance, you have to exercise a certain amount within a certain time and you have to do it regularly. Otherwise there's no point to it. A few laps in a pool every couple of weeks or a simple jog around the yard whenever you think about it isn't enough. Discipline yourself to follow a schedule. Find out how much someone your age and in your condition should swim or run, how many laps or miles in how many minutes. Then do it. When this regimen no longer tires you out (it won't after a while), increase the number of laps or the distance you run. Don't kill yourself. You're not training for the Olympics. But if you don't feel spent when you finish your exercise, chances are it's not doing you much good.

If you'd like to read more about swimming or running, there are hundreds of books on the subject. Here are a few of the better ones:

The Editors of *Sports Illustrated, Sports Illustrated Swimming and Diving* (Philadelphia: J. B. Lippincott, 1973).

James Fixx, *The Complete Book of Running* (New York: Random
    House, 1977).
George Sheehan, *Doctor Sheehan on Running,* new ed. (Mountain
    View, California: World Publications, 1975).

If you want to know more about aerobics generally, try *The New
Aerobics* by Kenneth H. Cooper (New York: Bantam Books, 1970).
Or, also by Cooper, *The Aerobics Way* (New York: Bantam Books,
1977).

Strength

So you're all set to exercise but you can't find a pool. It's too cold
to go running. You don't have an hour to spare. You're on a business
trip, staying in a small hotel room. *Now* what do you do? How can you
get some good, quick exercise?

Try push-ups and sit-ups. These timeless calisthenics may sound
old-fashioned. But they're still the best exercises for strengthening
your arms and your waist—the parts of your body that usually need
it most. Of course, as with all exercises, you have to do enough of
them. You also have to do them fast enough; otherwise they'll have
little effect. Gradually work your way up to fifty sit-ups and fifty
push-ups. That's right, fifty. More if you can. Even a hundred won't
take you more than half an hour a day.

The only trouble with calisthenics is that they aren't enough.
They're great for your arms, but they don't do anything for your heart
or lungs. When you finish them, you still need to run or swim or en-
gage in some other endurance-building exercise. Even if you do them
by the hundreds, push-ups and sit-ups are only a supplement to a well-
balanced exercise program.

Of course, if you're willing to put the effort into it, and if you have
a masochistic streak, a *very* rigorous and varied program of calisthenics can suffice. But to make it work, you'll have to spend several
hours a day doing chin-ups, pull-ups, leg lifts, and so on, as well as
push-ups and sit-ups. If you enjoy that kind of punishment, then you

deserve it. If you like the efficiency of calisthenics and you want to make them a part of your exercise program, try the regimen in *Royal Canadian Air Force Exercise Plans for Physical Fitness* (New York: Simon and Schuster, 1976).

If it's sheer strength you're after, isometrics are for you. They're simple and quick, and they require no space or equipment. All they require is your own body. You simply pit one muscle against another. Place your hands together, for example, palm to palm. Put your elbows out so your arms form a straight line in front of you, then press—as if you're trying to crack a nut. Hold the position, pressing as hard as you can, for fifteen to thirty seconds, then relax. Repeat. It may sound simple, but it's hard work and it will leave your muscles limp with exhaustion—a good sign. Isometrics can also be done using stationary objects or a partner.

We've saved weight lifting for last.

Weight lifting is fine, but if you only have time for one kind of exercise, it shouldn't be weight lifting. Like calisthenics, it's good for strength and muscle tone. In fact, it's particularly good, better than calisthenics, for muscle *definition*. But it does almost nothing for your heart and lungs.

However, if you're already doing something for your heart and lungs and you're looking for an exercise to improve your looks, try weight lifting. There's nothing wrong with cosmetic exercise as long as you're doing something else for your health.

Unlike calisthenics or isometrics, weight lifting requires equipment —hundreds of pounds of it. Don't buy it. Look for a health spa or gym near your office or home. Most of them offer free sessions that let you test the facilities and get to know the people.

If you've never considered yourself an athlete, or if it's been a long time since your athletic days, the prospect of going to a gym may be a little frightening. Like many people, you may have bad memories of locker room smells and the embarrassments of gym class. Take heart. You'll be pleased to discover that most commercial gyms are clean and inviting. The personnel are usually courteous and even helpful to newcomers. They won't laugh at how little you can lift or snicker at your modesty in the shower room. That kind of petty cruelty is peculiar to adolescents.

You'll also be pleased to discover the pace of your progress. If you like pumping iron enough to stick with it, within a few weeks you'll be proud of what you're lifting *and* proud of the change in your appearance.

A note of caution. If you don't know what you're doing, weight lifting can be dangerous. You can lift too much, too early. You can omit the important stretching exercises before you begin. You can inadvertently drop 500 pounds on your toe (or your head). Make sure you learn to use the equipment properly: how you should lift weights, how much you should lift, when you should add more.

If you're a beginner, the safest and wisest thing is to use a weight-lifting machine. Look around for a universal gym or the newly designed Nautilus system. Inexperienced weight lifters who use individual weights without instructions (at home or in the gym) are dangerously suicidal.

Even if you find a machine, get some instruction. Corner the trainer or take along a friend who already knows what he's doing. That will turn the session into an enjoyable social event as well.

Finally, don't overdo it. You don't want to look like Arnold Schwarzenegger. You certainly don't want to spend eight hours a day trying to. Weight lifting shouldn't become a fetish. It doesn't take more than forty minutes, three times a week, to keep you looking and feeling your best. You may even come to find it relaxing—an enjoyable way to unwind. After spending a long day at the office mindlessly pushing paper, it's a relief to spend forty minutes mindlessly pushing iron instead.

Flexibility

So now your biceps are bulging and you can run to the next state. Unfortunately, you can't bend down to tie your shoes. *Flexibility* is the third and last crucial ingredient in any balanced exercise program.

If you want more flexibility, find a good set of stretching exercises and stick with it. The best stretching systems, like the cheapest cars, are imported from the Far East: Yoga, Tai-Chi, Akido, Karate, and Judo, to name only a few. A good book on yoga is *Yoga Self-Taught* by Andre Van Lysebeth (New York: Barnes and Noble, 1973). If you want something that doesn't come equipped with a philosophy, try one of the Western systems, like the one developed by the venerable Jack LaLanne.

Flexibility is a worthy goal in itself. But whether or not you want it, it's important to begin any exercise with a few stretches (there are different stretches for different sports). Doing them is the best way to avoid jogger's knee, tennis elbow, and other athletic injuries. They may carry status in some communities, but they're hardly worth the inconvenience and the pain.

We repeat: It doesn't matter what exercises you do. Just make sure the ones you do produce the results you want. If you don't enjoy them at first, *learn* to enjoy them. The exercise you need to stay healthy and attractive will require a lot of effort and therefore a lot of motivation. The only sure way to sustain the effort is to enjoy it.

Posture

Stand up straight. This advice may sound as if it came out of a Boy Scout manual, but don't belittle it. Good posture is crucial to your appearance.

Always stand and sit erect. We don't mean you should look like you're strapped to a board. Ramrod posture is affected. But don't slouch either.

You should also walk erect. The Italians have a word for a man's personal style of walking. They call it his *vendatura*. Think about it for a moment. What's *your* vendatura? Does it convey the right impression? Can you be proud of it? Few things are more commanding than an energetic, authoritative, even athletic walk. Few things are more pathetic than a lazy shuffle.

Don't overdo it, of course. Walk, don't strut. Hip swinging is for boom-boom girls. Stick your chest out too far and you'll look pretentious, not self-confident. Don't bounce either. Teenagers bounce.

Finally, remember that good posture, like good grooming, eating right, and exercising right, *can* be learned. After all, *no one* knows how to walk when he's born. Doing anything right is only a matter of discipline and habit. Decide what you want to do and then plant it firmly in your mind. Think about it. Keep an eye on yourself. Correct yourself when you lapse into an old routine, when you start to slouch or you're tempted by a piece of chocolate pie. Keep this up for a few months and a miracle will happen. Discipline will become habit. You'll start doing the right thing automatically. Your new style will become truly a part of *you*.

For More Information

Clayton R. Meyers, *The Official YMCA Physical Fitness Handbook* (New York: Popular Library, 1975).

Nutritive Value of Foods (U.S. Government Printing Office, Washington, D.C. 20402).

U.S. Senate Select Committee on Nutrition and Human Needs, *Dietary Goals for the United States* (U.S. Government Printing Office, Washington, D.C. 20402).

PART THREE:

At Home

CHAPTER FIVE:

Designing Your Home

Designing Your Home in Style

You may think furniture is something only women need to worry about. Not so. If you're still a bachelor, for example, you may not have a woman around to guide the furniture selection or interior design. But, whether you do or not, you should know enough about the subject to help yourself. Think of your furniture as an extension of your clothing, and you'll soon realize how important it can be to creating and maintaining your style.

There are many different kinds of furniture. Unfortunately, most of them are in bad taste, in very bad taste. But just enough of them are in good taste to make generalizing difficult. Rules of furniture buying tend to be either too specific to include all the good or too general to exclude all the bad. Nevertheless, in a few pages, we'll do our best. We'll give you some do's and don'ts that will help you buy the kind of furniture that appeals to you most.

The Bauhaus Look

The Bauhaus was a school of design—for architecture, furniture, and crafts of various kinds—that originated in Germany after World War

I. The designers at the Bauhaus had two sensible ideas. First, good designs should be easily reproduced so everyone can afford them (no hand-carved furniture). And, second, good designs should take advantage of machine technology. It isn't honest to design machine-made furniture as if it were made by hand.

As you can see, the two ideas worked together. If you could use new machine technology to create good designs that everyone could afford, you could kill two birds with one stone. And that's exactly what the people at the Bauhaus proceeded to do. They created ideas for buildings, furniture, and objects that could be easily assembled from prefabricated machine-made parts. They stripped their designs of all traditional ornaments. They developed, instead, a new taste for simplicity. As they put it at the time, "form follows function"—if you want to make something look great, all you need to do is to figure what the item *does*, and then make it as simple as possible with simple materials and no frills. If you do, the object will be beautiful —beautiful and *cheap*. Cheap enough for everyone to buy.

In a few short years, men like Mies van der Rohe and Marcel Breuer designed some of the most beautiful furniture ever created using this philosophy. You've seen some of them countless times. The Barcelona chair, for example, the elegant chair in leather and chrome that Mies designed for the German Pavilion at the Barcelona World's Fair in 1929. Fifty years later, you can see the same chair in countless office buildings and homes. The Marcel Breuer Ceska chair and Wassily chair are other examples. Their tubular chrome construction has been imitated again and again. These enduring designs were the masterworks of Bauhaus furniture.

Unfortunately, things didn't turn out exactly the way the designers at the Bauhaus predicted. For one thing, the "masses" contrived to buy at Sears, so the designs were reinterpreted in expensive materials and sold to the rich instead. The whole philosophy of the Bauhaus was turned on its head.

In recent years, however, something has almost made the Bauhaus dream come true. You can still buy the Bauhaus masterworks at expensive prices from manufacturers like Knoll of New York. But if you're willing to settle for slightly less careful craftsmanship, you can find good copies of the masterworks at very reasonable prices. The Marcel Breuer Ceska chair, for example, is available for $50 (even less if you really hunt hard). Admittedly, $50 is not cheap for a chair, but you can't find much that costs less, even at Sears.

If you want to furnish your home stylishly, it's hard to think of a style that gives you as much elegance for as little money as the Bauhaus style. Of course, if you have it, you can always spend more. Remember, the Bauhaus look in furniture, like the American look in clothing, is the *classic* look. And, because it's the classic, you can't go wrong with it.

Three Bauhaus Furniture Plans

By themselves, the Bauhaus masterworks may be too severe or too costly for you—especially if you're just getting started with apartment living. So we've put together three Bauhaus furniture plans, one for a strict budget (you just started your job and your boss took an instant dislike to you), one for a comfortable budget (you've impressed your boss's boss), and one for an affluent budget (you just got your boss's job).

Each plan includes a few masterworks that you can keep and add to as your budget grows more generous. But even the other, less expensive pieces—the ones you'll want to discard gradually—are well within the spirit of the Bauhaus School.

The Beginning: Style on a Strict Budget

1.	Sleeper, brown corduroy	250
2.	Sisal rug	50
3.	White round formica table	75
4.	Four Marcel Breuer armchairs, natural color	300
5.	Two white laminate bunching tables	125
6.	White five-drawer stacking unit	100
7.	Standing lamp	75
		$ 975

Into Your Career: Style on a Comfortable Budget

I. Living Room

1.	Sectional sofa covered in white	$1,000
2.	Sisal rug	100
3.	White laminate square cocktail table	150
4.	Standing lamp	200
		$1,450

II. Dining Room

1.	Chrome and glass table	$ 300
2.	Marcel Breuer dining room chairs, natural color (two armchairs, four side chairs)	350
		$ 650

III. Bedroom

1.	Queen-size bed with mattress, box springs, and stand	$ 400
2.	Haitian cotton bedspread	100
3.	White laminate lamp table	125
4.	White laminate dresser	350
5.	Table lamp	75
		$1,050

The Ideal Setup: Style on an Affluent Budget

I. Living Room

1.	Parsons sofa, custom upholstered in dark gray	$1,500
2.	Parsons love seat, custom upholstered in dark gray	1,000
3.	Two Wassily chairs, black leather	500
4.	Mirror chrome coffee table	200
5.	Two mirror chrome end tables	1,000
6.	Wool carpet, medium gray (12 x 18 feet)	750
7.	Two standing lamps	400
		$5,350

II. Dining Room

1.	Glass and chrome dining table (42 x 72 inches)	$1,200

2.	Glass and chrome server (30 x 60 inches)	750
3.	Eight Mies van der Rohe dining room chairs	3,500
4.	Wool carpet, medium gray (9 x 12 feet)	750
		$6,200

III. Bedroom

1.	Queen-size bed with mattress, box springs, and stand	$ 400
2.	Wool bedspread	100
3.	Two Parsons love seats, custom upholstered in white canvas	2,000
4.	Barcelona coffee table	850
5.	White laminate dresser	500
6.	Two white laminate lamp tables	250
7.	Table lamp	125
8.	Wool carpet, medium gray (12 x 18 feet)	750
		$4,975

Quality and Expense

If you shop around for the pieces we recommend, you'll soon discover that the same piece of furniture—or what *looks* like the same piece of furniture—can have many price tags. For example, you can find a Wassily chair at Knoll for $720. You can find it at other stores for $540, $360, $280, and even $99.

Are these the same chair? No, not really. The Knoll version is considered to be the "original," meaning it's the version authorized by the designer. And undoubtedly, the Knoll version is made with greater care: fine leather, flawless chrome, and careful fitting and finishing.

But you *can* get a first quality piece of furniture for less than the top price. Of course, you can also get a piece of junk. If you don't want to play the risky game of bargain hunting, you can always buy from a reputable manufacturer like Knoll, and pay the price. If you're willing to take some chances, however, or if you can't afford not to, here are some tips to make your search less risky.

Sometimes poor quality just stares you in the face. For example, if you find a version of the Wassily chair for $99, it probably isn't made with real leather. It's probably made with leatherette. This is a sacrifice of quality you shouldn't be prepared to make.

There are other clues. Check the stitching on the leather. Is it even and strong? Check the chrome, too. It should be triple-plated, meaning the steel has been chromed three times. Chrome should be bright and shiny. If it's dull and shadowy, you're looking at inferior merchandise.

As for the Breuer dining room chairs, make sure the wood is of good quality, and make sure the pieces are dove-tailed, not just glued together. Dove-tail joining makes a piece of furniture much stronger. Also check the caning to see how it's been inserted into the wood. If it looks slap-dash, it may come out within a few months. Check to make sure the chrome tubes are each one piece, not two pieces joined under the seat. Make sure the stoppers at the ends of the tubes are chrome, not plastic. The rattan on Mies van der Rohe dining room chairs also varies a lot in quality. Compare several examples before you buy a cheaper one.

The hardest furniture to inspect for quality is padded furniture, sofas, chairs, and beds in particular. The quality depends on the strength of the wood frame, the tension of the coil springs, the thickness of the padding, and the quality of the upholstering—both fabric and workmanship. You can see the upholstery, of course, but you can't see the insides of the sofa or chair unless the store has a sample ripped apart to show. If it doesn't, you can only check a sofa or chair for comfort by sitting on it. The time to rely on brand names or store reputations is when you can't see what you're getting.

The purpose of all this checking is to ensure that you end up with a piece that will last as long as you want it to last. After all, you're buying classics. By definition, they're designs you'll never tire of. You may move them out of the living room to make space for newer, more expensive pieces, but chances are you'll find another place for them in the den or bedroom. The point is clear: Choose your furniture carefully, with an eye to the future, and you'll always be able to use it.

In Case You Don't Like Glass and Chrome

If you don't happen to like glass and chrome, all our recommendations so far may leave you cold. You may be thinking that Bauhaus is fine for airport lounges and hospital waiting rooms, but it's not what you had in mind for a *home*. Instead of glass and chrome, you were thinking of something in wood and cloth.

Well, take heart. While we may prefer the pure Bauhaus look of glass and chrome, we have to admit that you can have a striking and stylish room without them. Just be sure that you observe the Bauhaus hallmarks of good materials, simple designs, and quality craftsmanship.

Scandinavian Furniture. For example, try Scandinavian furniture —furniture made in Scandinavia or based on Scandinavian designs. It's usually made of wood—*all* wood, in fact—but it doesn't have the ponderous and bulky look of most contemporary wood furniture.

But be careful in choosing it. Part of the reason that Scandinavian furniture went out of fashion after its enormous popularity in the fifties was that there were so many bad examples of it around. They're still around, so pick your pieces carefully. The lines should be graceful, but not dainty or fragile-looking.

The Light-Wood Look. Scandinavian furniture has its problems. It's hard to find good pieces, and when you do, they're extremely expensive. To make matters worse, you can't really buy it in inexpensive versions—unlike the more traditional Bauhaus masterworks.

So if you want modern and you want wood and you can't afford to spend a fortune on furniture, try some of the contemporary designs in light-colored woods: maple, birch, elm, and oak. These pieces are relatively inexpensive, mostly because they're manufactured in the

United States. They're made with thicker wood, straighter lines, and more substantial legs than Scandinavian furniture, but their light colors keep them from appearing too bulky. This is a special benefit to the small apartment dweller who needs all the visual tricks he can get to keep his room from looking like a storage area.

To give you an idea how to substitute wood and cloth for chrome and glass, here again is our list of furniture for style on a comfortable budget—this time with a list of alternatives that might be more to your taste.

Glass and Chrome	*Wood and Cloth*
1. Glass and chrome table	1. Maple butcher-block table with chrome legs, 36 x 72 inches, $300
2. Dining room chairs	2. Prague chairs, natural color, six armchairs @ $100, $600
3. Lamp table	3. Two-shelf elm nighttable, $100
4. Dresser	4. Triple elm dresser, $325

The Look of Antiques

The Barcelona and Wassily chairs may be *modern* classics. But the real classics, the pieces that have *already* withstood the test of time, are antiques. Even the elegant lines and rich materials of a Barcelona chair can't match the two-hundred-year-old grace and personality of a Chippendale chair or Queen Anne sofa. So if you don't like the stark Bauhaus look—and many people don't—if you prefer lustrous woods and individual designs to industrial materials and the machine esthetic, consider antiques.

You may think only the rich can afford to buy antiques. Not so. You do have to have *some* discretionary income, but not as much as you might think. If you want to become a serious collector—that is, if you want to buy a couple of pieces a year—then you should count on spending at least $2,500 annually. That's a lot of money, of course, but it certainly doesn't restrict the antique market to Rockefellers.

In making the financial calculation, don't forget that antiques are an investment—one of the surest investments in the art world. If you buy a brand-new sofa, it will lose at least half its value the minute it leaves the store, no matter how much you paid for it. If you buy an antique, on the other hand, it will not only keep its value when you take it home, it will actually *increase* in value with each passing year. When you tire of that new sofa, you'll have to pay somebody to haul it away. When you tire of your antique, *if* you tire of it, you can sell it easily, sometimes for two or three times what it cost you. Antiques are good-looking *and* good business.

Reproductions

Reproductions are denfinitely not good business. In fact, it's difficult to understand why people choose to buy reproductions of antiques instead of real ones. It's true that some reproductions are very beautiful. But even the best are never as beautiful as the real thing. A fine piece of wood actually improves with age. Years of oiling and rubbing give it a rich lustre that simply cannot be reproduced in a new piece. Antiques, like people, have character. Reproductions never do.

Of course, reproductions still might make some sense if they were less expensive than original antiques. But in general they're not. A good reproduction can cost almost as much as the genuine article. Anyone who can afford a reproduction Chippendale chair by Kittenger (the largest manufacturer of first-rate reproductions) can probably afford a real one.

Yet reproductions, unlike antiques, have very little investment value. For all the care that goes into making them, they're really just like any other piece of contemporary furniture. Their value drops sharply as soon as they leave the showroom.

Later in this chapter, we recommend that you avoid interior decorators. This is especially true if you like antiques, or think you might. Why? Because interior decorators, as a rule, will do what they can to steer you away from antiques and toward reproductions or other contemporary pieces. Not for esthetic reasons, but for economic ones. Decorators are paid a commission on the furniture they sell you by the manufacturer. Antique dealers, on the other hand, generally give smaller commissions or don't give them at all. Buy a $1,500 reproduction and your decorator gets a bundle (as much as 50 percent). Buy a $1,500 antique and he may get nothing. Decorators are not fools. Don't you be either.

How to Buy Antiques

How you should buy antiques depends on how much you know about them. Experts can buy from a variety of antique dealers and auctioneers, although, as a general rule, most collectors work through one or two dealers with whom they've developed a relationship over the years.

If you're a novice, the best advice is to establish this kind of relationship with a good dealer. Buying antiques is no simple business. You have to *learn* how. It takes years of reading, shopping, and buying before you can rely entirely on your own instinct. In the meantime, the best way to learn is to apprentice yourself to the best dealer you can find.

How do you know a dealer is a good dealer? How do you know he won't try to unload that "authentic" Chippendale television console on you? The best way is to check his credentials with a friend who collects antiques or with other dealers in the area. Ask a dealer in a related field—an art dealer, for example. Another good source, maybe the best, is the furniture curator at your local museum. Ask a variety of sources who the best dealer in your area is and chances are the same names will keep coming up.

What to Buy

When you buy an antique, you buy a one-of-a-kind item. For us to tell you which antiques to buy would be like telling you which car to buy—not which *kind* of car, but which specific car rolling off the production line.

Obviously, we can't do that. But we *can* tell you what's available, what's generally good, and what you should watch for when you buy. As long as you observe some general rules, selecting an antique is basically a matter of personal taste.

English. English furniture has long been the darling of board rooms and country clubs, especially Chippendale, Queen Anne, and Regency. According to the laws of supply and demand, strong demand has driven the price of English antiques very high. The fact that there is, naturally enough, an absolutely fixed supply of English antiques has put the best English antiques out of almost everyone's reach.

But, curiously enough, the supply of English antiques is *not* absolutely fixed. In fact, making eighteenth-century English furniture has remained a lucrative trade in England right up to the present. That's right. A large percentage of English antiques are reproductions sold as originals. They're *fakes*, some so good that they've entered the trade as real antiques. A few are really antiques, in the sense that they're more than 100 years old. But they're old reproductions of *older* furniture—nineteenth-century reproductions of eighteenth-century originals. Antique fakes.

The upshot is that there is a lot more English antique furniture in England and America today than there was furniture in antique England. We don't say this to discourage you from buying English antiques if you can afford them. We just think you should be on your guard. Remember, wherever the values are higher, the number of fakes is too. It's at times like this that a good dealer is essential. The largest dealer in English antiques is Stair & Co., with showrooms in London, New York, and Palm Beach.

French. England has produced a great deal of fine furniture in the past three centuries, but the best furniture ever made was not made in England. It was made in France for the French royal families during the reigns of Louis XIV, Louis XV, and Louis XVI. For materials, craftsmanship, and design, you have to go out of the Western world, to Ming China, perhaps, to find comparable quality.

Of course, all this may be of slight interest to you if you're looking for a cabinet to put your records in. You may be willing to spend several hundred dollars on a Chippendale piece, but not $15,000 for a Louis XVI commode. Fair enough. We can even emphasize the point by reporting that the world auction record for a piece of furniture was set in December 1974 at Sotheby Parke-Bernet in London for the Lady Baillie Louis XVI desk. Price: a mere $552,000.

But if you've got a penchant for high French furniture, and you've got the wherewithall, by all means investigate the market. We recommend you start your search at Rosenberg & Stiebel, Inc. in New York.

But we don't want you to think that the French royal family was the only family in France that used furniture. Things may have been bad before the Revolution, but not that bad. In addition to French royal furniture, there's French Provincial—not pseudo-French Provincial, the delicate stuff you often find in new-furniture stores, with lots of curves painted white and gold in imitation of royal French furniture—but real French Provincial, heavy, large, made of unpainted wood, and usually manufactured for French country homes. This kind of furniture is not only attractive but much, much cheaper than the more ornate variety.

American. American furniture is certainly not as sumptuous as the finest French furniture, and probably not as chic as the best English pieces, but it *is* significantly cheaper and easier to find. We also think that American furniture, at its best, rivals the furniture of any country in design. In short, it's a bargain for antique collectors.

The most helpful book on American antiques is *Fine Points of Furniture: Early American* (New York: Crown Publishers, 1950) by Israel Sack of Israel Sack, Inc., the foremost dealer in American furniture. Sack takes three different examples of the same item from different periods and tells how they differ in quality. He explains why, for example, three different Philadelphia sidechairs vary so much in quality and value. It's an excellent way to learn about antiques without the risks of buying them.

Be Consistent

Once you're bitten—and the lure of old furniture is irresistible—be consistent in your selection. Obviously, how eclectic you can be in your buying will be determined, to some extent, by how many rooms you have and by how big they are. But there are certain styles that just won't go together. For example, Louis XIV furniture (lots of straight lines) won't mix with Louis XV (lots of curves). Mixing French Imperial furniture with American colonial will make your apartment look like the props room on a movie set. Don't make these mistakes. Pick one style or pick the other, then stick with it.

How Much Should You Spend?

How much you should spend obviously depends on what you plan to buy. If you're in the market for remnants from the palace of Versailles, you'd better have a palatial budget. If you want the best examples of eighteenth-century English or American furniture, you'll need to spend at least $5,000 a year. But you *can* buy fine antiques on half that. Find the right period for your budget.

Seventeenth-century furniture, out of fashion since the 1920s, is still affordable and very beautiful. Look carefully and you can pick up a great item for relatively little. Empire furniture (France, 1804–1815) is becoming more fashionable, which means it's becoming more expensive. It's still affordable, but don't wait too long. Sheraton, Hepplewhite, and Federal furniture are generally less expensive than Chippendale or Queen Anne.

But why not be brave? Why not look at some of the furniture that museums and collectors are only beginning to buy? Your bravery might net you some spectacular items at reasonable prices. Look, for instance, at Renaissance Revival furniture from the 1870s, 1880s, and 1890s. Or the furniture of the Arts and Crafts Movement in America (1876–1916). These are the pieces you can buy now for practically nothing—or look back on ten years from now and wonder why you didn't.

The important point, regardless of your price range, is to buy the best item you can afford. As you'll see in the next chapter, the same rule holds true when you're buying works of art. A great work from an unpopular period or by a neglected artist is a wiser investment than a mediocre work from a chic period or by a famous artist. It's also probably a better piece of furniture.

The Balanced Look

The third style we recommend is hard to describe. We call it the "balanced" look. It's distinguished by simple, unpretentious, comfortable furniture, with an emphasis on good materials and careful craftsmanship. It's more modern than antiques, but more traditional than Bauhaus.

We should tell you right off that there are two basic problems with the Balanced look. First, it's the most difficult to put together well. Unlike the Bauhaus style, it involves any number of colors and patterns. Mixing them successfully is as difficult as mixing clothes. More difficult, actually, since there are no formulas to follow. It's not easy to assemble a variety of different pieces into a harmonious whole without resorting to the restrictions—or at least the assistance—of a set of rules.

Unfortunately, the Balanced look will also cost you a lot of money. Remember, we said the emphasis was on good materials and careful craftsmanship. Well, neither has ever come cheap. The Balanced look may cost less than the look of antiques, but it certainly costs more, sometimes much more, than the Bauhaus equivalent.

Despite these difficulties, we would guess that the majority of Americans prefer the Balanced look. So what follows is an attempt to make this difficult goal a little easier to reach: a brief guide to meeting and mastering the challenges of the Balanced look.

The Heritage of Antiques

The Balanced look is based remotely on a mixture of French, English, and American antiques. But when you look at it, you don't see its distant heritage. The style is essentially English—or is it? There's a close kinship, certainly, but the lines are straighter, heavier, more modern. The relationship may not be pronounced enough to *see*, but it's one of the reasons why Balanced furniture mixes so successfully with real antiques. They're all in the family.

The kinship of Balanced furniture and real antiques is so distant and subtle that we can safely say, if you can *see* the kinship, don't buy the piece. If it looks like an antique—even vaguely—chances are you're getting a bad reproduction, not a good Balanced piece.

Steer clear of modern interpretations of antiques. They occupy an esthetic no-man's land: They're not antiques, they're not reproductions, they're not Balanced. They're just *bad*. We're talking about *any* contemporary piece labeled "French Provincial," "Mediterranean," or the like. These designs have nothing to do with either France or the Mediterranean. They were invented in Grand Rapids by a manufacturer who was trying to give you what you *think* looks French or Mediterranean. His French Provincial has lots of curves in white and gold (*real* French Provincial is heavy, rough-hewn, and brown). His Mediterranean has knot holes and heavy iron fixtures (a little closer to the mark, but not much).

Of course, *some* French Provincial and Mediterranean furniture is better than others. The versions you buy from Henredon, for example, are better than the versions you buy from Sears. But it's *all* bad. The same is true of Colonial furniture. Some colonial pieces come close to being reproductions. Most don't. If you buy any, make sure you know the difference.

Used Furniture

If you want simple, well-constructed furniture—in other words, if
you want good Balanced furniture—try a used furniture store. That's
right, *used* furniture. Of course, we're not talking about the second-
hand stores that sell the same stuff we just discouraged you from
buying, only this time "used" because the person who made the
mistake in the first place couldn't keep up the payments. We're also
not talking about antique stores that mark the price up several hundred
percent the minute a piece celebrates its hundredth birthday.

We're talking about the furniture stores that fall between these
two. Stores that carry furniture usually made within the last fifty
years by reputable companies and workshops for private and commercial use. The people who run these stores make it their business
to know when an old building is being torn down and its furnishings
are going up for auction; when the probate court is selling furniture
to satisfy a person's debts; when another furniture store is going out
of business. If you're looking for bargains in fine furniture, this is
where they're made.

These bargains won't require any sacrifice in quality either. Look
carefully and you'll find first-quality pieces in solid woods, exquisitely
crafted in every conceivable style. Searching for a good heavy desk,
vaguely Chippendale, preferably mahogany, for your office? Buy it
new, and you'll spend $2,000 at least. Find it in a used furniture
shop (recently extracted from the president's office of an old bank
building), and you'll pay a quarter to half as much—for a *better*
piece of furniture. As long as the previous owner took reasonably good
care of it, the wear and tear will only give it more character.

Used furniture stores may be the best places to find these bargains,
but they're not the only places. If you're watchful, you can find the
same auctions, garage sales, and court-ordered sales that the dealers
find. If you do, you'll pay only a fraction of what the dealer would
charge you. But unless you can make it a full-time pursuit, you're

probably better off letting the dealer do the legwork. Even with his mark-up, you'll get a first-rate piece of furniture for a song.

Colors

We said earlier that the Balanced look is a challenge. Once you forsake the simplicity of the Bauhaus look—white walls, neutral colors, minimal decoration—the variety can be overwhelming. Suddenly you've got to worry about colors that harmonize and patterns that don't clash. Textures, shades, accents, and on and on—on the walls, on the floor, on the drapes. Abandon the Bauhaus and you open a Pandora's box.

The trick is not to abandon the Bauhaus principles completely. Less is still more. For example, in choosing colors, stick to a few. You don't want a lot of different colors in a room, especially if any of them are strong. Avoid the rainbow effect of bright red walls, pink drapes, bright blue sofa, and purple chairs. If it *sounds* bad, it will always look worse. Instead, select a single, basic color for a room. Use other colors for accents only. If you're having trouble getting colors to harmonize, just leave one out.

Don't get carried away. Too much—even of a good color—is too much. A prominent interior decorator has a bad habit of filling his rooms with red: red walls, red drapes, red sofa and chairs, red flowers in a red vase on a red table on a red shag rug. What isn't red is purple-red or orange-red or some other frightening variation. What he wants to do, of course, is knock you off your feet. He succeeds admirably.

For the same reason, you should avoid any color in a strong hue, unless you know exactly what you're doing. A deep blue can look all right if it's well chosen, but chances are you'll tire of it much more quickly than you would tire of a pale beige. Finally, under all conditions, but especially if you're a bachelor, avoid a color scheme of red and black.

Patterns

Discretion is also the better part of patterns. In general, the best patterns are modest ones. A small diamond pattern is better than a large one. Thin stripes are generally better than wide ones. You want a pattern to provide a subtle, unexpected interest, not to rivet your attention the moment you step into the room. Keep two rules of size in mind. The larger the *piece*, the more restrained the pattern should be. The larger the *room*, the bolder the pattern can be.

Avoid patterns that look artificial. Geometric ones are safest. Floral patterns are fine, but avoid any attempts at three-dimensional realism. A floral pattern is printed on a two-dimensional fabric, and it should look that way. Above all, avoid artificial animal skins. Nothing looks worse than a fake tiger- or zebra-skin throw pillow— and you find them surprisingly often among otherwise tasteful furnishings.

As a matter of fact, avoid *genuine* animal skins as well—especially if you didn't catch them yourself. Wild animal skins used to be signs of virility. Now they're a sign of indifference—indifference to the survival of endangered and often beautiful species. It doesn't matter how good that tiger skin might look on your floor next to the fireplace. It looks a lot better in the jungle—alive. Leave it there.

Mixing patterns is even more difficult than mixing colors. But the same principle holds: Keep them to a minimum. Never more than two or three strong patterns to a room.

Instead of mixing patterns, try mixing textures: tightly woven fabrics with loosely woven ones, smooth fabrics with rough ones. As in everything else, don't get carried away. Avoid an abundance of furry fabrics, nubby fabrics, or anything else that looks a little eccentric. You don't want every visitor running her hands over the furniture or rolling around on the carpet. There are better places for running and rolling. A collection of textures isn't necessary. A few will suffice to give your furnishings the subtle variety you want.

Quality

As with any other style, you want the very best items you can afford
when you assemble a Balanced room. The richest woods, the finest
fabrics, the warmest hues. A well-oiled, beautifully-grained mahogany
is far more impressive than a profusion of bright colors. A plain
fabric beautifully woven from a natural material like wool or silk is
far more impressive than a cheaper fabric printed with an ostentatious
floral design. Choose a variety of rich materials and you won't have
to manipulate colors or patterns to achieve the *effect* of richness.

Unfortunately, if you really want rich colors and intricate patterns,
you may have no choice but to buy the best. Paint your walls a·rich
crimson, for example, and you'd better use the best paint on the
market. You'd also better have enough money left over to do the
job again if the shade doesn't turn out right. This is the risk—and
the price—of being bold.

The same principle applies to patterns. A good patterned carpet
is much more expensive than plain wall-to-wall. A fabric with a good
floral design is much more expensive than plain cotton. The advice
is clear: Don't experiment with rich colors and intricate patterns
unless you've got the money, time, patience, and persistence. If you
don't, the plainer the better. Stick to white walls and plain fabrics
in simple colors (beige, gray, brown, dark blue), and you can put
together a room that's just as stylish, at a fraction of the cost, with
a fraction of the effort.

The Danger of Over-Coordination

We've made such a point about coordination and harmony that we'd
better mention the opposite danger, over-coordination. It may sound
strange, but you can put together a home or apartment that's *too*
tasteful to be in good taste.

What does it mean to be too tasteful? For one thing, it means that the colors or patterns are too well-coordinated. Nothing is worse than a room that's all one color, except, perhaps, a room in which *selected items* are the same color. If you have crimson curtains, a blue carpet, and a blue sofa, don't go out and buy crimson pillows for the sofa. The effect will be well-organized, all right, and deadly.

It's much better to be a little eccentric, as long as everything harmonizes. Not matches, harmonizes. You want everything to go together, but you don't want it to go together *too* well. You want to strike a balance between coordination and contrast.

Putting It All Together

Once you've chosen the furniture, carpet, patterns, and colors, you still have to put them together. A room can be filled with fine objects and rich materials and still not work as a room. Think about what goes with what, and what goes where. In fact, you'd be well advised to make those decisions before you start buying.

Mixing Styles

We've given you three styles of furnishings to choose from: Bauhaus, antique, and Balanced. But we don't mean to give you the impression that you have to stick with a single style. Just the opposite. You may want to combine a thick, stuffed, Balanced sofa, a Chippendale sidetable, and a Wassily chair in the same room. Mixing styles is not only acceptable, it has some distinct advantages.

For one thing, using a few Bauhaus pieces in an antique setting can lighten the room. The chrome and glass can keep the heavy wood antiques from making a room look too somber or formal. On the other hand, Bauhaus furniture isn't as comfortable as it might be. A good heavy, stuffed sofa can provide a lot of comfort in a room otherwise furnished in the Bauhaus style. Not just physical comfort, but visual comfort, so the room doesn't *look* too stark. Antiques, too, mix well with any style. They can provide both the Bauhaus look and the balanced look with more personality than either style possesses on its own.

Arranging Your Furniture

If you have trouble arranging your furniture, chances are you have too much of it. But even when you're down to the bare necessities, there isn't as much choice in arranging them as you might think.

Less is More. Most people have too much furniture. Their homes or apartments resemble furniture stores: They're difficult to walk around in and cluttered to look at. Most people could throw away half the furniture they've accumulated over the years and never notice the loss.

This is especially true if you live in the city. City dwellers need as much space—psychic *and* real—as they can get. Cluttering up your apartment with unnecessary furniture is not the way to get it. Selecting a few good pieces and placing them carefully *is.*

So why not look through your furnishings and see whether you can edit anything out? Is that cluster of tables really necessary? That trunk in the corner covered with a tablecloth? That standing lamp you never use? Keep what you need, of course, but throw the rest out. Remember, the less furniture, the better.

What Goes Where? If the room is large, arrange the furniture in "islands." The number of islands will depend on how much furniture and how much space you've got. Each island should consist of a sofa, several chairs, and a table or two arranged in a conversation group. Obviously, if the chairs don't face each other, conversation will be difficult. One way to separate the group from the rest of the room is to arrange it on a separate carpet.

If filling a large room is your only problem, consider yourself lucky. For most people, the problem is not having enough space. The solution is to follow a clear-cut procedure. First arrange the

various items by size (in your mind, that is). Then look at the walls
in the room. Always start with the largest piece of furniture, probably the sofa. Put it against the longest uninterrupted wall. Then
take the largest chair and put it against the next longest wall. Continue the process until you've placed all the major pieces.

Avoid placing furniture in traffic lanes or in the middle of the
room. But don't line it all up along the walls, either. Visitors will
think you just vacuumed. As a general rule, the smaller the space,
the less you want to interrupt it. Don't try to divide a small room by
running bookcases, couches, or tables across the middle of it.

Follow these basic rules and you can't go wrong. In fact, you won't
be *able* to think of a better way. The right arrangement is the inevitable arrangement.

Be Your Own Decorator

The American Design Institute isn't going to like us for saying this,
but you're probably better off *without* the help of interior decorators.
Most of them went to school, all right, where they learned about
patterns, colors, arrangements, and so on. But we'll risk a broad
generalization and say that most interior decorators do more harm
than good.

Why? Precisely because they learned *too much* about patterns,
colors, arrangements, and the rest. Most of them end up putting twin
pillows on your sofa made from the same material as your drapes.
Most of them are guilty of the sin we've talked about: being too
tasteful for *your* own good.

It's cheaper, much more enjoyable, and probably safer to trust
your own educated taste.

Background: Walls, Floors, Windows, Lights

The background for your furniture—whether it's Bauhaus, Antique, or Balanced—should be as simple as possible. We're not sug-

gesting that if you're fortunate enough to live in an old building with high ceilings and heavy moldings you should scrape the walls bare, lower the ceilings, and paint everything white. By all means, take advantage of the setting.

But if you're among the vast majority of people who live in simple rooms with plain walls, we certainly advise against adding elaborate period details. Paint the walls white. If your furniture is Bauhaus, the rule is absolute. White. All white. No ivory, buff, lace, bone, egg-shell, off-white, or any other compromise. After all, the Bauhaus style is a pure style, and white is the purest color. Besides, you'll find that white makes everything else in the room look better—the furniture, the carpets, the paintings, the other works of art, even the people—no matter what your preference in furniture.

If your house or apartment has good wood floors, you're in luck. Just have them stripped and refinished. If you prefer wall-to-wall carpeting, it should be a neutral color—beige or gray.

The less you have on your windows the better. Venetian blinds are great for the Bauhaus look, although they're difficult to keep clean. The 1-inch variety is much more elegant than the 2-inch. If you're striving for the Antique or Balanced look, you want drapes. Just remember that nothing makes a room look smaller than dark, heavy drapes at the windows.

We've recommended lamps in case your home isn't equipped with overhead lights. But if they're already there, or if you want to put them there, go right ahead. The best solution is track lighting, a series of lights on a track that can be moved along the track and swiveled in any direction. Track lighting has obvious advantages for lighting works of art, but it provides good, even light throughout a room whether or not you have works of art to light. The best track lights are the simplest ones—white and cylindrical. You don't want chrome details or colors of any kind.

If you need a centered overhead light—over a table, for example, or in an entrance hall—the best kind is a factory or hospital lantern, which is shaped like a very broad funnel. Again, as always, white is best.

Oriental Carpets

You should consider buying one or more Oriental carpets. Use them instead of the neutral carpets we recommended above and you'll give your room instant color and personality.

How do you select an Oriental carpet? Our advice is this: If you can afford to spend a lot of money, go ahead and buy a new one. Otherwise, you're much better off buying an old carpet. Or—if it has to be new—buy a tribal carpet, instead of a carefully crafted one. (Never, of course, an "Oriental" carpet machine-made in Belgium or Japan.)

Tribal carpets may look rough to you at first, but they're relatively cheap and much more honest than the touristy red Bukharas manufactured by the thousands in Pakistan and India. In fact, *most* new Pakistani and Indian carpets should be avoided. The colors are too bright. The wool is inferior. The finish is smooth and shiny. They're just badly made. Not roughly made like tribal carpets, but *badly* made. The designs call for a standard of craftsmanship the manufacturers can't afford to meet. The result is a carpet that looks shoddy when you buy it and that will look only shoddier with age.

You'd be surprised how inexpensive and how good an old carpet can be. We don't mean an antique, of course. But we don't mean a carpet that's only a couple of years old either. It can show some wear. It might even be worn through in spots. Just make sure that its fibers are still strong and rot-free. You'll find that old carpets have some definite advantages. Their colors are often mellower, the designs more authentic, and the workmanship superior. You can find old carpets in the same stores that sell new ones, or occasionally, at auctions and garage sales. If you're lucky, you can fill a large room with an old oriental carpet for as little as three or four hundred dollars.

Accents

You want the background elements of your apartment—the walls, floors, window coverings, and lights—to be as simple as possible because simple means elegant. But there's another reason, too. A simple background will show off the items that give your apartment or house its personality. If you've got white walls and neutral-colored carpeting, there's nothing for the colors in your paintings or furniture to compete with. And they're the colors you want to see *most*. In fact, you'll find that a really simple background can make a work of art look even better than it is. It takes a great painting to compete successfully with an intricately designed wallpaper. But even a modest poster or print can look impressive against a white wall. Create a simple backdrop for your personal things and you'll be doing them a big favor.

Art will probably provide most of the accents for your house or apartment. But we're using a loose definition of the word "art" here. A simple setting will show off paintings to their best advantage. But it will do the same things for antiques too: a gilt mirror, an American quilt, a collection of porcelain, or just about anything else. These are the things you want to look at and you want other people to see.

Plants can also provide an interesting accent, although, as a rule, you don't want to put them on display. Don't fill the room with them (unless it's a conservatory), and don't put a full-size rubber tree in a small one-room apartment. A few good-sized plants are better than a herd of little ones, crowding the table tops and competing for the air. Also, since plants are alive and should stay that way, make sure you can take care of them. A good print is better than a brown and withered vine.

Knickknacks

Avoid knickknacks whenever you can. That's all there is to it. An attractive room is simple and uncluttered.

Of course, it may be impossible to avoid knickknacks altogether. Like everyone, you accumulate possessions that, for one reason or another, have sentimental value. Photographs of the people you love, interesting ash trays you've picked up on a vacation somewhere, whatever. If they're too sentimental or too personal, be sure you keep them out of regular public view. Photographs of family and friends, for example, should be displayed in your bedroom, not your living room.

You also have possessions that you happen to be using at the moment. You can't always be bothered to put them away the minute you stop using them. A book you're reading, the jacket of a record you're listening to, a sweater you just took off. All these things will keep your house or apartment from looking like a museum. That's as it should be. A *few* knickknacks are not only permissible, but mandatory. They're a sign of life.

For More Information

Terence Conran, *The House Book* (New York: Crown Publishers, 1974).

Charles W. Jacobsen, *Oriental Rugs: A Complete Guide* (Rutland, Vermont: Charles E. Tuttle, 1962).

Marvin Schwartz and Betsy Wade, *The New York Times Book of Antiques* (New York: Times Books, 1972).

Hans M. Wingler, *Bauhaus* Translated by Wolfgang Jabs and Basil Gilbert (Cambridge, Massachusetts: MIT Press, 1969).

Chapter Six:

Buying Art

Buying Art in Style

Back when only royalty did it, it was called "patronizing" the arts. When the new rich joined in, it was called "collecting" art. Now it's simply called "buying" art, and anyone can do it. Whether it's a Monet painting for the parlor or a poster to cover the bare spot in the hall, art has become a part of almost everyone's life.

Of course, it still helps to be rich, especially if, like most people, you have a taste for French Impressionist paintings. But more and more, the successful man is buying art and building his own "collection." The process is usually gradual, starting with only a print or a poster. At first he may not even think of it as building a collection. It's really more like decorating. But as his position and income advance, he starts adding original works: sculptures, paintings, rare prints. Before long his collection, like his career, has become rich and varied.

Why is art, so long the exclusive realm of royalty, suddenly available to everyone? Primarily because there's just more of it around. More artists doing more works in more different kinds of materials. The results, of course, are mixed—variations in price *and* variations

95

in quality. But the fact remains that there is great art out there in every price range, just waiting for the knowledgeable buyer—whether he has visions of opening his own gallery or of just covering that hole in the wall. It's only a matter of deciding what you like and how to go about acquiring it.

Is Art a Good Investment?

Let's get one thing straight. Most of the time, art is *not* a good investment. Occasionally you'll pick up a newspaper and read that someone just made a million dollars selling a painting he bought for a few hundred. But the fact is, you have about the same chance of making that much money in the lottery as in the art market.

In fact, it's been estimated that less than 1 percent of the works of all living artists ever increase in resale value. Even if yours are among the lucky one percent, you still have to find a dealer to sell a picture for you, and then you have to pay him about 20 percent of the profit. You also have to consider the problem of inflation: A picture's value has to increase a little just to keep up with it. Very few works of contemporary art increase enough in value to bring the owner a profit when he resells them.

The same is true of older art. An older work increases dramatically in value only if the supply goes down suddenly or the artist's reputation rises suddenly. Neither happens very often. In fact, studies show that the art market isn't really any more lucrative than the stock market.

Art's only advantage is that it's more of a pleasure to own. Paintings will look much better on your wall than stock certificates. The main point is to buy art because you like it, because you want something attractive on your walls, not because you expect it to increase in value. Of course, if it does, so much the better.

What Not to Buy

Before we list the kinds of things you might consider buying, we want to start with a few warnings about what you *shouldn't* buy. The task is an easy one. Precisely what you buy will depend on your personal tastes. Just remember that there are several kinds of "things" that call themselves art but aren't.

Schlock Art

The one thing you should avoid at all costs is Schlock Art. You've seen it. Pictures of small children with big eyes. Sail boats drifting into a scarlet sunset. Kittens, puppies, flowers. Anything that's cloying and sentimental. Unlike genuine art, Schlock Art is not hard to find. It's in the home departments of most large department stores, in theater and hotel lobbies, and in special "galleries" thrown up in malls and shopping centers with a sign that says something like "ART FROM AROUND THE WORLD."

But it isn't just the subject matter or the selling place that makes Schlock Art schlock. The works themselves are bad. Real bad. Garish colors and slap-dash brushwork. Take a look at any work by LeRoy Nieman, the famous sports "artist," and you'll know what we're talking about.

Schlock art is sometimes made by famous painters. More often, it's made by moonlighting commercial artists or, even worse, by factories of destitute art students that employ assembly-line techniques: one "artist" paints the sky, another the waves, and a third the sailboat. The result: truckloads of practically identical works polluting the world at a rate of $60 for a "sofa-sized" picture.

One final warning. Schlock Art doesn't have to be new. It's been around as long as the entrepreneurial spirit. So don't be tricked by the age of a work. If you can't yet distinguish Schlock Art from the serious stuff, think twice before spending *any* more money on art.

Limited Edition Art

In recent years, several manufacturers have capitalized on the new crave for collecting by issuing "limited" editions of mass-produced art objects. Porcelain birds, Christmas plates, religious and commemorative medals, presidential plaques, coins in silver and gold. According to the advertisements, they're designed or sculpted by professional "artists" and sold on an installment basis—one a month for a decade or two.

Beware. These are not works of art. They're sentimental curiosities and very few of the "artists" responsible for them are worthy of the name. Like the word "art," the word "limited" is used loosely. The editions are limited, all right—to the number of people, who *want* them. The company sends out the publicity, counts the orders, *then* sets the limit. It can be fifty or 50,000. Often the numbers are so high that the word "limited" loses all real meaning.

There are two main reasons to limit an edition. First, it allows items to be checked more carefully for quality. Second, it ensures sufficient rarity to preserve artistic uniqueness and investment value. Limited edition manufacturers may check for quality more carefully than Ford Motors, but they provide about the same level of artistic uniqueness. The investment value of limited editions is based on the notion that there are people who *want* the object but can't get it because it's so rare. Obviously, if an item is "limited" to everybody who wants it, its investment value is zero. In short, buying limited edition art makes no artistic sense and less financial sense. Spend your money elsewhere.

Reproductions

If you can't afford to buy major paintings, why not buy photographic reproductions to hang on your wall?

We'll tell you why. Think for a minute about what you get when you buy a reproduction. It's a *picture* of a painting. So much gets lost in the translation. It's probably not the same size as the original. The colors are never exactly right. It doesn't have any of the *feel* of the original; the brushwork is lost. In fact, a photograph of a painting is about as good as a photograph of a person. It may remind you of what the original looks like, but it certainly can't take its place.

Some reproductions are, of course, better than others. For obvious reasons, large paintings with rich colors and complicated brushwork reproduce the worst. Small, black and white drawings on paper reproduce best. Sculptures, too, are somewhat more successful than paintings, especially when careful attention is given to reproducing the surface finish and patina of the original. Some reproductions also cost a lot more than others; they range from $15 for a small print of Monet's *Waterlilies* to $1,500 for a gold-leaf, full-size facsimile of the caryatid from Tutankhamen's tomb.

But a reproduction is a reproduction. We suggest you avoid them at any price. Even the expensive ones rarely look right. There's simply no way to make a brushstroke look like a brushstroke without a brush. Photographic reproductions just won't do. Even when reproductions are at their most successful—as in the case of Nelson Rockefeller's reproductions—even when they trick you into believing that you're looking at the real thing, the whole effort seems wrong-headed. It seems wasteful to put that much time, energy, talent, and money into reproducing works of art that already exist when the same resources could be invested in creating new ones.

The other problem with expensive reproductions is that they're expensive. Fifteen hundred dollars for the reproduction of a figure from Tutankhamen's tomb is a *great deal* of money. Less than the original, by a long shot. But the original will continue to increase in value. The reproduction won't.

If you have that much to spend on art, why not buy an original? It's enough to buy a fine one. A small landscape by an American Impressionist, for example. A large sculpture by a living artist who's building his reputation. Or a print by a major artist you've always liked. Any one of these would be a better object and a better investment than a reproduction.

Where To Start

Starting an art collection requires nothing more than a little money and a bare wall. For many people it begins with the simple urge to "put some color on the wall" or "liven up the place." It would be snobbish (as well as mistaken) to deny that all art—even great art—is also decorative. Yet many people seem to think that they can't have both decoration and fine art, especially when they're just starting to buy and don't have much to spend.

The surprising truth is that you can have both from the very start—from the first poster in your apartment to the Gainsborough in the board room. All you have to do is know where to look and what to look for.

The Work of Younger Artists

If you want to start with contemporary art, but you can't spend a couple of thousand dollars, look at the work of younger artists. Actually, we don't mean "younger," we mean *unknown.* Unknown artists can be any age. What they really have in common is obscurity, which is why their works are relatively inexpensive.

How inexpensive? You can spend as little as $800 on a large painting by one of these artists. Drawings will cost substantially less. Even this may sound like a lot of money to cover a wall, but you have to realize that the dealer is getting about 40 percent and the artist probably doesn't sell very many works. If you can spend that much, you can rest assured that the money really *means* something to the unknown (and probably starving) artist.

Of course, buying the work of younger artists is more difficult and more challenging than buying the work of famous ones. For one thing, you have to trust your own taste. If you want some help, you might look first at the less expensive artists who sell their works through reputable dealers. The fact that a dealer shows the artist's work means that at least one expert thinks it's good. You might also check to see whether a museum has exhibited the artist's work. That's another expert assessment.

But the best approach is to cultivate your own eye. Once you've done that, your taste should be your guide.

Prints

Given a choice, almost everyone would prefer to collect major works by the old masters or the Impressionists. But only a few can afford to pay $1 million for a Rembrandt. Even $30,000 for a Robert Motherwell is beyond the reach of most of us. But what about $1,000 for a Motherwell print? Or $500 for an Alex Katz print? Or $250 for a print by Frank Stella? Of course, $250 is a lot of money. But it's relatively little for a work of art by a great artist.

In fact, if you are willing to accept a less-than-great impression, you can often find prints by the greatest old masters for that amount— even by Dürer or Rembrandt, two of the greatest artists ever to work in the print medium. Prints make it possible for many of us to collect art by the kinds of artists we really *want* to collect.

What exactly is a print? A print is a work of art, usually on paper, that's reproduced from another surface—a wood block, a metal plate, a slab of stone. Most prints are published in an *edition* of more than one, although there are also a few *monotypes* in which the entire edition consists of a single print.

Obviously, since every print is made separately and every one is made by hand, some versions—or "impressions"—are better than others. When you're assessing a print, check the materials first: the clarity of the ink, the texture of the paper. The quality of the printing is also important: Are the margins complete? Is the impression sharp?

Make sure you buy an *original* print, not just a reproduction. Normally you should be able to tell the difference by looking at the bottom of the work. If it's numbered and signed by the artist in the margin, it's probably a print (you should check the back, too, where some artists prefer to sign). If not, it's just a glorified postcard, not a work of art.

Of course, the signature itself doesn't always mean something. Some artists have confused the issue by signing reproductions. But in most cases, the signature means that the artist has personally supervised the making of the print.

As always, the best precaution, if you don't feel confident to assess the originality of a print yourself, is to find a reliable dealer. After all, an important part of any dealer's job is distinguishing the worthy from the worthless. To find a reliable dealer, ask a representative of the Art Dealers Association or of the local museum.

Here are the major galleries that sell contemporary prints in New York and elsewhere:

New York:
  Brooke Alexander, Inc.
  Castelli Graphics
  Getler/Pall
  Pace Editions
Boston:
  Harcus Krakow Gallery
Chicago:
  Richard Gray Gallery

Los Angeles:
  Margo Leavin Gallery
Minneapolis:
  John C. Stoller & Co.
Philadelphia:
  Makler Gallery
San Francisco:
  John Berggruen Gallery
Washington, D.C.:
  Fendrick Gallery

A note about artists to avoid. People who buy modern prints for the first time are often drawn to the fame and superficial charms of Marc Chagall, Salvador Dali, or Victor Vasarely. In fact, these are names to avoid.

There's a widespread myth that money and success destroy modern artists. As a matter of fact, the myth is usually false. But in the cases of Chagall, Dali, and Vasarely, it happens to be true. All three created great works at some time in their careers. Examples to see and admire can be found in many museums, particularly the Museum of Modern Art in New York City. But after an important early career, each artist —to put it bluntly—fell apart. Each artist began to rework earlier ideas in new, increasingly boring pictures. The same is true of their prints. Avoid them.

Joan Miró is an artist who has occasionally made great prints throughout his career but who has also turned out dozens of weak ones along the way. Unless you know exactly what you're doing, you might want to avoid him as well.

Art for $250 and Less

Art doesn't have to be expensive. In fact, it can be very cheap. Here are some ideas of what you can buy for less, maybe much less, than $250.

Photographs. Photographs by important artists such as Stieglitz and Atget can cost thousands of dollars. But you can get a fine photograph by a leading contemporary photographer for between $100 and $250. Photographs like these can often be purchased directly from the photographers themselves. Otherwise, you can generally find their works at the same galleries that sell contemporary prints (see our list) or at galleries that specialize in photography.

But you don't even have to spend $100 to $250 to get a photograph that will look good on your wall. Unless they were taken by a major photographer, most old photographs can be purchased for only a few dollars. Any photograph that's at least fifty years old has some historical interest, regardless of the photographer. Many have some esthetic interest as well. It will cost more than a few dollars to get the photographs framed. But, especially if they're well chosen, the cost is well worth it.

Posters. *Reproductions* are discouraged, but *posters* definitely are not. Many posters *include* reproductions, but there is usually some type on them too. The type keeps the posters from trying to look like the original. That makes them more honest than reproductions. Old movie posters, art exhibition posters, political posters—there is a wide variety.

Antique Objects.   Real antiques are, by definition, more than 100 years old. Actually, objects don't have to be quite that old to have an antiquarian appeal. While a genuine Louis XVI table can cost you several hundred thousand dollars, a fine old crockery jug can cost as little as $20. Antiques are less risky than anything else you can buy. Nothing at least 100 years old is in terrible taste. Some objects are obviously superior to others, but none of them is an embarrassment, which both photographs and posters often are.

Old Prints and Drawings.   Unless, of course, you have your heart set on a signed drawing by Rembrandt, or something equally out of reach, you can buy a print or drawing by an older master, sometimes an important older master, for $250 or less. A print or drawing that any museum in the world would be happy to have in its collection. A print by Jean François Millet, for example, one of the most important Realist artists of nineteenth-century France, or a drawing by Francesca Alexander, the nineteenth-century American Pre-Raphaelite artist and a favorite of John Ruskin.

The problem with all these items—photographs, posters, antiques, and prints and drawings by old masters—is that what you buy is only as good as your eye. You can buy a great work of art, a mediocre one, or a disaster, depending on how well you've trained your powers of discrimination. As we've said, the best way to learn is by making mistakes. So don't wait until you've gained full confidence before you start buying. Gain your confidence by trial and error. But remember, too, that the more time you spend studying art—especially the kind you intend to buy—the better you'll do in the art-buying world.

Presentation

After you've bought something, whether it's a poster or a painting, there are still the problems of where to put it up and how to put it up. A good installation can improve the appearance of even the most modest work. A bad one can kill even the best. You need the right wall, the right frame, the right lighting, and, above all, the right position. Presenting your pictures calls for almost as much care as acquiring them.

Framing

A bad frame can ruin a good picture. But good frames are expensive. It's hard enough to spend a lot of money on a frame for an expensive print or picture. Doing the same for a modest purchase (for the kitchen wall, perhaps) is almost impossible. But *necessary*. In fact, you may end up paying as much or more for the frame as you paid for the picture, especially when you're shopping for inexpensive prints and posters. But get used to it. Settling for a cheap frame is a little like buying an expensive suit but getting a pair of cheap shoes.

Here's the basic rule: Don't buy a work of art until you can afford to frame it properly—regardless of how much the work itself costs.

What do we mean by "frame it properly"? There's no sure answer. It depends on the work of art. The only general rule is, the simpler the better. A simple gold frame works best on most traditional prints. If you don't feel confident about selecting the frame yourself, call your local museum and ask them to recommend the best framer in the vicinity. Then ask the framer for his advice.

For most prints and other works of art on paper, two kinds of frames work best: stainless steel frames welded at the corners and chromed on the front edge, and molded plexiglass frames. Any good framer has them or can order them for you.

What about the metal frames that you assemble yourself? These never look as good as the kind that are welded together at the corners. They are adequate, however, for photographs and small works of art on paper. If you use them, use only the thinnest frames, and use only silver or white, never brass or any other finish.

Also, don't buy nonreflecting glass. It cuts the reflection all right, but it also cuts the light. That's enough to kill the work of art.

Matting and Conservation

The frame isn't the most important aspect of displaying photographs or works of art on paper; the mat is. Mat board is made from two different materials: wood pulp and cotton rag. Whenever you have a work of art matted, *be certain to ask for four-ply 100 percent rag matting.* You have to *ask* for it. It's more expensive than the other kind, so if you don't ask for it, the framer will almost always give you a mat made from wood pulp. Matting that has rag sheets on either side of a wood pulp filler won't do. It's got to be *all* rag—both the masking board *and* the back board.

Why is this so important? Because wood pulp has acid in it that destroys paper. The higher the wood pulp content, the more acid. That's why newsprint—which is 100 percent wood pulp in content—self-destructs in a few months. Mats that have even the slightest wood pulp content will begin to self-destruct after a few years. And that's only the beginning of the trouble. The acid will eventually seep into the work of art and destroy it, too.

In addition to using rag matting, there are several other rules important in conserving all works of art on paper. Know them, and insist that your framer follow them carefully. Insist, first, on water-soluble hinges to attach the work of art to its backing. Masking tape won't do.

Second, make sure that the work of art doesn't touch the glass or plexiglass of the frame. A mat is usually sufficient to accomplish this. If you're not using a mat, ask the framer to *recess* the work. Finally, if you plan to hang the picture in a room that receives bright sunlight, ask for U.S. 3 plexiglass, a variety that shields the picture from harmful ultraviolet rays.

What color should a mat be? The simplest and best answer is white. You can't go wrong with a white mat. The *only* exception is an off-white mat, which can be used for older works of art printed on off-white paper. Nothing is worse than a brightly colored mat, or a dark one. Use one of these, and you won't see the work of art; you'll only see the mat.

Hanging

During the nineteenth century, the fashion was to hang a lot of pictures on the same wall, in clusters. But no longer. Today, unless you're hanging family photos, it's better to hang only a few good pictures.

That makes things a lot easier, too. Clusters are hard to arrange. Arranging several pictures on a single wall is almost as difficult as arranging the various forms in the composition of a painting. You practically have to be an artist in your own right to do it correctly.

But even hanging a few pictures can be difficult. Here are a few rules:

First, compare the size of the picture with the size of the wall you want to put it on. If the picture is nearly as big as the wall, put it directly in the center. (Use a measuring tape; none of us has eyes that accurate.) If it's considerably smaller than the wall, put it off-center.

Hang the paintings or prints at eye level. You want to be able to look at the paintings when you're standing up without straining your neck up or down. Many people mistakenly believe that all the paintings on a single wall should be even at the top or the bottom. This is only true if the paintings are about the same size. If they are, the bottoms, not the tops, should be aligned.

Check to see whether there's a dominant direction in the painting. If it's a portrait, for example, does the figure face one way or the other? If it does, make sure you hang it so that the face looks toward the center of the room, not toward the wall. This may sound picky. But if you're not careful, the picture will look "crowded."

There's a special warning about works of art on paper. They fade easily. Hang them on walls that don't receive direct sunlight. When you buy a work of art, you're accepting the responsibility of keeping it in good condition. That's one of the many ways in which surrounding yourself with art—even inexpensive art—differs from mere decorating.

For More Information

William M. Ivins, Jr., *How Prints Look: Photographs with a Commentary* (Boston: Beacon Press, 1958).

H. W. Janson, *History of Art*, 2d ed. (Englewood Cliffs, N.J.: Prentice-Hall, 1977).

Cecile Shapiro and Lauris Mason, *Fine Prints: Collecting, Buying, and Selling* (New York: Harper & Row, 1976).

George L. Stout, *The Care of Pictures* (New York: Dover, 1948).

PART FOUR:

At Work

CHAPTER SEVEN:

Designing Your Office

Working in Style

Style is success. When you're stylish, you're successful. That's why style is important—perhaps most important—at work. Whether it's right or wrong, men with style tend to surpass their less stylish competitors. They win quicker promotions, enjoy better office relations, and make better impressions on their clients. In short, they're successful.

Putting your style to work for you is not hard. And it's definitely profitable. The only trouble is, in most working situations you don't have a lot of independence in defining your own style. After all, the firm has its own style—the company image—and you have to develop your personal style within that image. Otherwise, the company image would be in chaos: every employee dressing differently, decorating his office differently, or dealing with colleagues and clients differently.

But once you get to the top, there's more breathing room. When you're the president of IBM, for example, you'll have much more freedom in designing your office than the trainees in your sales department. A man who owns his own firm can shape his own style—as well as the firm's—with complete freedom.

Well, not exactly *complete* freedom. In the end, even the top executive and the self-made man have to conform, if not to the organization's image, then to the expectations of the business community and their clients. If they want their businesses to prosper, both the president of IBM and the founder of a chain of stores must conform somewhat to society's image of the way responsible, level-headed businessmen look and behave. But they also want to appear as stylish as they can within the limits of this image.

When you establish your working style, you want to do what's right for your career *and* what's right for your style. In most cases, striking the right balance between success and style is no problem. In most cases, they're the same thing.

First Things First

People form their impressions early. Before they meet you, before they even step into your office, visitors arrive at your building, locate your office, and speak to your secretary. All these experiences tell them what to expect when they finally do meet you. It's important to create the right mood from the first.

Location

The location of your office has a lot to do with its prestige—and yours. Unfortunately, there's not very much you can do about the location of your building in the city, except, perhaps, lobby for a move to a better neighborhood. But there is often something you can do about the location of your office in the building.

The position of your office in your building says a lot about *your* position in the firm. Prestige is generally established by three factors:

1.   Height in building. The higher the better.

2. Distance from entrance or elevator bank. The further the better.
3. Quality of view. The better the better.

But the *most* important prestige factor isn't location; it's size.

Size

Your office should be as big as possible. It's hard to imagine one that's *too* big. The greatest luxury you can have isn't a fireplace or a balcony or a bar. It isn't sumptuous materials or even a spectacular view. It's space, and the more the better.

The larger the office, the more comfortable it is. Not just because it can accommodate more furniture. Not just because you can walk around in it. It's more comfortable because empty space is comfortable. Americans are comforted to *see* space even when they're not using it.

Access

Anything is more alluring if it's hidden: a secret, the future, a woman's body.

The same is true of an office. A closed door is much more alluring than an open one. If a man keeps his door open, you can see him sitting at his desk doing precisely the same kind of work you do. There's no mystery in it. If he keeps his door closed, you might think he's engaged in an important conference, or working on a vital report, or making crucial decisions. So keep your door closed and keep them guessing.

In some offices you may not have the option of keeping your door closed. Office policy may prohibit it. Or your door may be glass. If you can't have the policy changed or the door replaced, you'd better get used to working in public.

Choosing a Secretary

An even better way to protect access to your office is to make visitors walk through your secretary's office on their way to yours. This is only possible if the offices are laid out properly, of course, but most executives' suites are. It's democracy's answer to the palace guard.

The most impressive secretaries are attractive. But that doesn't necessarily mean *young*. The most attractive secretaries are often middle-aged or even older, but they dress well, speak well, and carry themselves regally—all qualities you're not likely to find in a twenty-year-old ex-cheerleader.

A middle-aged secretary will also give your clients the impression, accurate or not, that you've had the same loyal and efficient secretary throughout most of your career. It's for this reason—and the fact that most older secretaries are *better* secretaries—that many top executives hire middle-aged women to take care of their offices. They know enough to keep sexual fantasies out of the file cabinets.

If you have more than one secretary, you can be more flexible. Try a variety of ages. Of course, there are *some* kinds of variety you shouldn't try. Some important senior executives have been known to choose secretaries by their hair color: at least one blonde, one brunette, and one redhead, all of them young and beautiful, of course. The result is not a staff; it's a harem. Some male visitors may get a thrill at the sight, but they may also doubt the employer's professionalism.

Incidentally, the highest status symbol isn't a pretty secretary; it's a secretary with a cultivated British accent. In Britain, just the opposite is true. American secretaries are the status symbol.

Before you hire a secretary, decide whether you need a secretary or just a receptionist. Never choose a secretary for her looks or her voice unless she also happens to be a good secretary. It's all very fine to have a pretty woman with a pleasing voice to greet visitors, but it also helps to have someone who can type. And, perhaps most important, someone you can get along with. After all, your relationship with your secretary is more like a marriage than an affair. Harmony is the essential ingredient.

Nameplates

A nameplate on the door tells visitors who is behind the desk inside. That's all it does or should do. Don't try to personalize your nameplate so that it says something about your personal style. Normally we're in favor of such statements, but not here. If everyone in a firm chose his own style of nameplate, the result would be visual chaos. An elegant nameplate system has to be a *system*.

That's the first important rule about nameplates. The second is that the more permanent and important a nameplate looks, the more permanent and important you'll look.

Permanent or removable, keep it small. Large nameplates are flashy and, like anything flashy, in bad taste. If you want a nameplate to broadcast the message that you're important, do it with the elegance of the materials, not with the size of the letters.

Where should a nameplate go? In one place, and only in one place: on the wall, two or three inches from the knob side of the door at eye level. If you do put it on the door, and you keep the door open, people won't be able to read the nameplate until they're already inside the office. And that's too late to do them much good.

In Your Office

Unless you happen to be president of your firm, chances are you won't have much say about the location of your building or office, the choice of your secretary, or even the selection of the nameplate on your door. But one important prerogative you probably will have on your way to the presidency is the opportunity to furnish your office, to choose the kind of furniture that suits your own tastes. Here are some pointers for furnishing your office stylishly, whatever your tastes happen to be.

Less Is More

The less you have in your office, the better, for two reasons. The first is esthetic. Unless you can reproduce the sumptuousness of Versailles, it's far easier to achieve elegance with a few good pieces. That's the essence of the Bauhaus look, of course. But the same holds true for the look of Antiques and for the Balanced look. Whatever your taste, just remember the basic rule: A few good items are better (not to mention cheaper) than a lot of them.

But as you probably guessed, there's more to it than esthetics. A sparsely furnished office is an uncluttered office. And an uncluttered office is an organized office. This can be taken to extremes, of course. An empty room may look organized but it also looks unoccupied— a bad impression to give your boss. Just make sure there is no excess furniture. Your office should tell anyone who walks into it that you're in control of yourself, and in control of your business affairs.

Of course, the less you have in your office, the bigger it will look, as well. The feeling of space will add considerably to its prestige value.

Layout

Visitors step first into your secretary's office. Her desk should face the door so she can see and greet them without engaging in gymnastics. The typewriter should be placed so her vigilance can be maintained. Put the files within reach.

How you place your desk depends on your personal working habits. But there are some basic rules. *Don't turn your back.* Visitors should never be ushered in from behind your desk, no matter how much you enjoy the view. The desk should either face them as they enter or, in the best arrangement, face the side wall.

Don't face the window. Unless you have unusual powers of concentration or a particularly dismal view, your desk should never face the window. Whether or not the view distracts you from work, visitors will assume it does. Just as lawyers are supposed to avoid even the *appearance* of impropriety, you should avoid even the appearance of daydreaming.

Behind the desk should be a credenza, a long, low storage cabinet. It's basically an extra that provides extra storage space and extra desk top. If your desk has no drawers, a credenza may be essential. It can also be a logical place to store your typewriter or dictating machine when not in use. We don't necessarily approve of the practice, but if you or your clients need a midday nip, a credenza can double as a bar.

In front of the desk should be a straight-backed chair, facing the desk to facilitate conversation. It can be comfortable, but not too, because it's intended for brief conferences, not extended visits. A comfortable chair will only encourage a visitor to linger. For longer conferences or more welcome visitors, you should have a conference area.

A conference area is any place where two or three people can sit down comfortably and talk. It does not have to be large or luxurious and you don't need to be the president of General Motors to have one. Unless your office is a mere cubbyhole, it can probably accommodate at least two lounge chairs and a coffee table off in one corner —the basic conference area. If your office is relatively large, try several chairs and a couch, grouped, perhaps, on an area rug to set them off. If you *are* president of General Motors, try an adjoining suite with kitchen, dining room, bedroom, bathroom, and pool. Whatever your station, a conference area gives you flexibility in dealing with your clients. *You* can be more comfortable and you can make *them* more comfortable.

The Modest Office

If modesty is a virtue, then some offices approach sainthood—especially if you're a young executive in a fast-growing firm. While the Board battles over whether to rent four or five floors in that new, strike-delayed skyscraper, you're stuck in a converted broom closet. Or you're the victim of subdivision: One office is now four. Due to partitioning, your privacy may end at eye level; your conversations the subject of office gossip, your sniffles the object of office sympathy.

But even the most modest office can be designed according to the same principles as the most lavish. The only real difference is there won't be room for a conference area. Therefore, all conferences will be at your desk. If you use a straight-backed chair, regular visitors will dread their arrival and long for their departure. Not an attitude conducive to making friends and influencing people. So pick something relatively comfortable.

Also keep things in scale. A small office demands scaled-down furniture. Big desks may look commanding in large offices. But in small offices they look crated and ready to ship. Keep the bulk down. No great armoire-like cabinets. Keep the wood blond, the colors light, the chairs small, and the files in the next room.

Furniture

If it's good enough for your home, it's good enough for your office. So stick with the three styles we discussed in Chapter Five.

Only a decade ago, all conservative professions—business, law, banking—required conservative furniture along with conservative dress, conservative thinking, and conservative politics. We are happy to report that conservative furniture is no longer required. Today, sleek Bauhaus furniture fills the offices of even the most prestigious Wall Street bankers. The liberation is not complete however. There are still some holdouts. So if you want to play it real safe, keep the modern furniture in the modern businesses, like television, advertising, public relations. But in most places you can protect your status by buying only the best, regardless of the style you choose. A marble-topped desk with chrome legs may not make a traditionalist smile the way an eighteenth-century Chippendale desk does, but the money you spend on it will certainly win an appreciative nod. After all, the oldest and most venerable conservative tradition is money.

Whatever style you choose, here are some tips for furnishing your office:

The Bigger Your Desk, the Better. As long as it doesn't dwarf you or the room, that is. It's probably *too* big if people start asking how you got it through the door.

A Desk Chair, Not a Throne. Your desk chair should be moderate in size. Too small and it will look temporary; too large and *you'll* look temporary. At all costs, avoid huge, theatrical, black leather thrones. You'll resemble a small child sitting in a grown-up's chair. You know it's too big if your feet don't reach the floor.

The Light from Above. Whenever possible, ceiling lights should replace table or standing lamps. Avoid the burning-the-midnight-oil look of small desk lamps. Keep the room pleasantly light even on the cloudiest days.

Your Secretary's Office

Think of your secretary's office as part of your own. After all, it's the first thing visitors see, the first hint they get of *your* working style. Be as careful in designing it as you are in designing your own office.

Try to use the same materials: the same walls, floors, and window coverings. If you've been too lavish in designing your own office, this may be prohibitively expensive. If so, at least coordinate. Paint your secretary's office the color of your trim. Don't panel the walls, but use the same wood for mouldings.

Of course, there's one additional problem in decorating your secretary's office: your secretary. After all, it's her office too. Chances are she won't object to the color of the walls or the grain of the wood. If she has a thing for Bauhaus and you like traditional, she should expect to conform to your taste, and you would be right to insist on it. But you should think twice before banishing family pictures from her desk simply because "Less is more." Remember, esthetics seldom justify bad manners.

You should, however, convince your secretary to avoid the most glaring problems. Above all, you should establish that her office is not a three-dimensional scrapbook in which she is free to paste and tape a variety of postcards, pictures, and treasured quotations. If she considers this an unjustified invasion of her privacy, then maybe she should seek her privacy elsewhere.

Persuade your secretary that scotch tape is not the proper way to mount something on a wall. Offer to frame a print or poster that she particularly likes. Gently discourage those impressionistic, greeting-card posters of lovers, sunsets, oceans, children, kittens, and the like. You shouldn't dictate, but you can and should set standards.

In a modern office, the secretary's furniture should be made of Formica or enameled metal. The best colors are white for the Formica and buff for the metal. A light wood can also be used. The worst material—and, of course, the most common—is Formica done up to look like wood. Formica is fine, but it should look like Formica.

In a traditional office, a secretary's desk can be—although it doesn't have to be—made entirely of wood. *Real* wood, that is.

But there's an argument for using modern furniture in your secretary's office even if you use traditional furniture in your own. The argument involves file cabinets. Unless you can afford to have files custom made from elegant woods or built into paneled walls, modern file cabinets are essential. They're cheap, efficient, *and* attractive. But if the file cabinets are modern, the secretary's furniture should be too, otherwise you'll end up with an undistinguished mix. Purity—in whatever style—is always preferable.

Finally, an essential feature of any secretary's office, modern or traditional, is an IBM Selectric typewriter—preferably black.

On Your Walls

What if you're not president of your firm yet, or even vice president? What if you just graduated from professional school and started on the job? What if you were assigned your office and *given* your furniture? No one bothered to ask whether you prefer traditional or modern. What is left to display your creativity and style? Your *walls*. Unless your firm is draconian in enforcing its own style, you probably have some say in deciding what goes on your office walls. Make sure it says what you want it to say.

Diplomas

Diplomas were invented to decorate office walls. Except for the few moments when the president of your school hands it to you at graduation, the only real function a diploma serves is decoration. The truth of this is instinctual. Most people take their diplomas and head straight for the nearest framer. Once framed, the diploma goes onto the office wall—or into the attic trunk.

There are a few cases when a visible diploma may actually serve a function. A doctor, for instance, may want to reassure his patients that he did in fact go to medical school. A lawyer's clients might also be interested in knowing whether he went to law school.

But in general, parading your education is a bad idea. Only Harvard graduates do it regularly, and that's because nothing after college makes them feel as important as college did. Handle yourself well, be at ease in your job, and people will *assume* you had the "right" schooling. Act like a professional and you won't need a diploma to prove that you are one.

So if you're not a doctor or a lawyer, don't hang your diploma on your wall. Keep it rolled up in a closet to amuse your grandchildren. Or, if it's already framed, hang it in the den or basement. Some people make their comment about college education by hanging their diplomas in the bathroom. There are, undoubtedly, other creative solutions.

If, after all this, you still insist on hanging your diplomas, at least make sure you frame them properly. Avoid the thin black frames most people use; they'll dominate the diploma. Use a plexiglass, white enamel, or stainless steel frame instead. If your office is traditional, a simple gold frame is the answer.

Trophies and Other Mementos

You've probably seen offices filled with college trophies, football pennants, and school mugs. One Wall Street banker who went to Princeton and was proud of it, kept a stuffed tiger nestled at the foot of his desk.

Putting in eight or more hours a day, commuting an hour each way, and taking two or three weeks of vacation a year can make the college experience seem a lot better than it really was. Just compare life at work to life at school: skipping classes, getting three or four months of vacation, and living within five minutes of everything and everyone. It's easy to see why so many of us retain—or manufacture —such good memories of college, and why so many men display mementos of their college years, especially their college triumphs, long after those triumphs have faded.

However strong the urge to relive college in decorating your office is, resist it. Unless the mementos are related to your work, they'll convey the idea, accurate or not, that you'd rather be out on the playing field or back at the frat house than doing what you're doing. Save them for your den at home.

Obviously, this rule can bend a little depending on what it is you want to display. An Olympic gold medal or a Nobel Prize will win more friends and influence more people than an admirable but overly zealous adherence to strict principles of simplicity.

Political Photographs

It can be very impressive to walk into a man's office and see a dozen photographs of him smiling and shaking hands with former presidents, senators, and the like. Presumably, in order to get them he served in the government or had a lot of contact with government officials. Political photographs *can* be very prestigious.

But only if they're the real thing. To begin with, the politician in the photograph must be recognizable. Any former president will do, more or less. Senior Cabinet members, popular governors, and sena-tors also make the grade. An obscure congressman or local official doesn't. A sports figure would be better.

Second, it must be apparent from the photograph that you actually *knew* the politician who's shaking your hand. Pictures with the two of you standing by yourselves or seated in discussion are best. At the other end of the spectrum are pictures that show you shaking the politician's hand in a receiving line at a high school gymnasium. Dis-card these.

One final note: too many autographed pictures, like too many of anything, can diminish the impact of each. Unless you're out to com-pete with Sardi's, the New York restaurant, limit them to fewer than a dozen.

Family Photographs

Why would a man want to put his family on exhibition in his office? Putting a family photograph in your office doesn't demonstrate your love so much as it violates their privacy.

Several books suggest that it can be useful to your career to display such photographs in your office. In fact, some businessmen *may* prefer to conduct business with a family man on the assumption that he must take his work more seriously. After all, he has a wife and kids to feed. Even if the assumption is accurate, which it probably isn't—most people have enough trouble keeping themselves fed—anyone who thinks this way can get the information he wants by looking at your finger. He doesn't need to see your wife and children smiling cheerfully from a cluster of photographs.

But, you say, there is another reason for keeping photographs of your family in your office. You may *miss* them, especially if you work a long day and commute a long way. Some lawyers and bankers in New York are known to go weeks at a stretch without seeing their youngest children, who are in bed asleep long before daddy arrives home from work. These men need photographs to remember what their family *looks* like. If this is your dilemma, pictures won't help.

A better solution might be to stop working so much and spend more time with your family.

The only way to display family photographs without displaying your family is to place them on your desk facing you, not your visitors. But it's better to avoid the problem altogether.

Works of Art

There's no better decoration for an office wall than a work of art. But keep two considerations in mind.

First, the work has to be good. When you make your choice, follow the principles we outlined in Chapter Six.

Quality is important, but so is appropriateness. There's a difference between buying a work of art for your home and buying one for your office. When you buy for your home, you only have to satisfy your own taste. As long as the work has artistic integrity, anything goes. But when you buy for your office, you have to be more careful. A silk screen of an electric chair by Andy Warhol is a fine work of art. You could hang it in your home without reservation. But at the office, especially if you're a lawyer, it could create quite a stir. You don't want your decorations raising damaging doubts among clients and colleagues, no matter how unjustified those doubts may be.

The safest works in this sense are generally abstract. There's no reason to restrict yourself to abstractions, though, as long as you use a little common sense in making your choice.

Books

If there's an empty wall in your office, you don't *have* to hang something on it. Try putting bookshelves there instead. If they are well bound, books can be as beautiful as works of art. And, like a good work of art, a well-stocked bookcase says something about your intellect. Despite television, most people in this country still respect people who read.

There's a danger, however, in having too many books. A professor should have as many books as his office will hold. He *wants* people to think he reads all day long. He wants people to be intimidated by his knowledge and erudition. But most other professionals want to avoid the reputation of a bookworm. The reputation of a *reader* is quite sufficient. In the end, professionals should be too busy working to spend very much time reading. Or at least so most people think.

The point is this: One bookcase will impress your visitors; two will put them off.

However many books you have, they should be related to your job. So assemble your work-related books at the office and leave your science fiction, Civil War history, and running manuals at home. Lawyers and doctors have an advantage. Their schooling left them with a ready supply of large, expensive, well-bound, and thoroughly useless books for display as decoration, decoration that inspires a lot more trust from their clients than any diploma could.

Rooms with a View

If you're lucky, your office may come with a ready-made decoration: a view.

Prestigious firms compete fiercely for the highest floor of a building because of the view. It stirs the heart to sit at a desk in a lower-Manhattan skyscraper and scan an aerial view of the Statue of Liberty and the gray Atlantic. Or, out the other side, New York, in all its polluted glory.

But city views are by no means the only impressive ones. Many large corporations have moved their offices out of the crowded city and into the countryside. The move reduces both taxes and commuting times. But another benefit is the view: grass, trees, and unpolluted sky. If you're lucky enough to have either the Statue of Liberty or a lush landscape out your window, you don't really need to worry about decorating your office. Just open the drapes.

Music

It is possible to decorate an office for the ear as well as for the eye. *Music* makes it possible. But before you pack up your stereo and take it to the office, consider the nature of your job and the nature of your firm. We've already talked about the need to conform to the corporate image. This is especially true when it comes to something as innovative as playing music while you work.

As a general rule, only men who work for liberal firms or who are highly placed in their firms have the option. But that very fact is part of what makes office music such a status symbol. So if you *do* work for a liberal firm, if you're highly placed in your firm, or, of course, if you work for yourself, consider decorating your office with music.

If the firm doesn't object, the only risk you're running is that music might bother your clients. They might consider it—and you—frivolous, more of a danger in business than in government, academics, or other walks of life. They probably won't, but if you're worried about it, turn the music off before your clients arrive. Or offer to turn it off when they arrive.

Still, with all the risks, try it. After all, several presidents of the United States have done it and been admired for it. What was good for their PR will be good for yours. Besides, music does create a pleasant working environment.

But what music should you play? The answer is simple. Classical. Nothing else. No rock, no jazz, no country western, no matter how much you like them. Save them for weekends. Also, no Musak, otherwise known as "elevator music," or else your office will sound like a hotel lobby.

Classical music is easy to listen to and, just as important, easy to ignore. There is also much less chance of offending a client's taste in music. No one is going to denounce Beethoven or Mozart the way they might denounce Merle Haggard or Dolly Parton.

Although all classical music is equally acceptable, some pieces are more equal than others. Generally, the fewer the instruments the better. A Beethoven symphony, for example, is a little monumental for the office. Have you ever tried talking over Mahler's Eighth? Big choral works (Mozart's C Minor Mass) or operas (Wagner's Ring Cycle) fall in the same category. In fact, you'll probably want to avoid all vocal music. The most suitable music, logically enough, is chamber music. Mozart quartets, Bach concerti, Beethoven piano trios, Brahm's anything.

The easiest way to listen to classical music while you work is to turn on a good FM classical music station. Most cities have one. Of course, if you listen to a radio, you have to take what they give you —Beethoven's Ninth as well as his piano trios. Not to mention announcers, advertisements, occasional talk shows, and other interruptions. If you prefer to choose for yourself, set up a sound system in your office. You can even have your secretary change the records or tapes for you.

On Your Desk

There's one place that you control regardless of your position in a firm. Whether you are president, vice president, or a recent recruit, your desk is your castle. How you keep it—cluttered or neat, full of gadgets or austere—tells any visitor a lot about your style, especially your working style.

Less Is More

The same rule for furnishing your office applies to furnishing your desk: The less you have on it the better. In fact, an *empty* desk is best! By empty, of course, we don't mean completely empty. A telephone is always necessary. And except when you're on vacation you presumably have the report you're working on and a few related materials.

An empty desk is neat, but we don't recommend it for the esthetics alone. An empty desk says something about you, and what it says is good. You may think a man with a desk piled high with papers, reports, and books looks like a hard worker. In fact, just the opposite is true. Clutter on your desk says you can't handle the work. Accumulated work gives the impression that you can't organize your time any better than your desk, that you certainly are not the man for *more* work in a higher position.

An empty desk, on the other hand, says that you have no trouble keeping up with your work load. Not because you don't have enough work to do, but because you do it so efficiently. A full desk means your affairs are in a jumble. An empty one means they're in order.

For the same reasons, avoid an in/out box if you can. Have your secretary keep it on *her* desk instead. That way people can't watch unanswered mail mount up in your box. You don't want your work rate to be the subject of office gossip.

Nameplates

Never use a desk nameplate if you can help it. Why? For the same reason you would never use a removable nameplate on your door. Both are removable, which suggests that you are too. They convey the impression that you probably haven't held your present job very long, and that you may not hold it much longer. Not because you're moving up, but because you might be moving out.

Blotters

What about a blotter? If your desk is modern in design, the answer is easy. Never use one. Nothing looks worse on a modern desk—whether it's made of Formica, glass, marble, or sleek wood—than a leather-bound blotter.

If your desk is traditional, then a blotter is acceptable although by no means mandatory. The most elegant ones are built right into the top of the desk. The writing surface is entirely covered with leather and often tooled in gold around the edges.

Unfortunately, a leather-top desk is more expensive than most of us can afford. If your desk isn't inset with leather, and you still want a blotter, just make sure it's made of good leather and that the design, if there is one, is appropriate for the desk.

Pen and Pencil Sets

Most people never actually *use* a pen and pencil set. They just put it on their desk for decoration. Like any other supposedly functional object that doesn't actually perform a function, it looks artificial, to say nothing of pretentious. It's best to do without one.

A man rarely goes out and buys an elaborate and expensive pen and pencil set for himself. He generally receives it as a gift from a friend, a business associate, or an employer. The gifts are often inscribed, making them difficult to pawn or pass along as presents. When this is the case, it's acceptable (and probably unavoidable) to keep the set on your desk. You don't want to offend the donor. Esthetic principles seldom justify bad manners.

The Telephone

A telephone should be beige, dark gray, or black. No colors, that is. Why? Because you want it to look as conservative as possible. Like a good waiter, a telephone should provide the essential service without being obtrusive. If you have a white Formica desk, however, a white phone is acceptable.

Keep away from anything too sleek. Princess phones are obviously out. In fact, the basic model is best. A Touch-Tone phone is better looking, though, and easier to use than the old dial variety. If you receive numerous phone calls, you may need more than one line. Many businessmen measure their success by the number of lines they command.

Other Gadgets

Your phone should be the only mechanical equipment on your desk. If you use a dictaphone or tape recorder, keep it to the side or in a drawer.

If you find it easier to write at a typewriter, go ahead and use one, but follow this simple rule: Never let anyone *see* you type. In fact, no one should ever even see the typewriter. Close the door when you're using it. Put it away when you're not. The major exception is in the publishing industry. Even influential New York publisher Clay Felker has a typewriter in his office. But prominent lawyers and powerful government officials who type well often keep their abilities secret even from their own secretaries.

The reason is that it can ruin a man's image as an executive to be seen typing. This is especially true for young men on their way up. Let the office know you can type and the next thing you know some-one (maybe even your boss) will be asking you to do a little typing on the side. It's a silly convention, we admit, but a crucial one. As we've said, some office conventions are vital even though they can't be justified on esthetic, moral, or other high grounds.

For More Information

Alan Lakein, *How to Get Control of Your Time and Your Life* (New York: David McKay, 1973).

CHAPTER EIGHT:

Presenting Yourself

Presenting Yourself in Style

Think of yourself as a puzzle. Everything you do or say, everything you own, everything that has your name on it is a piece of that puzzle. Ideally, each of the pieces should be attractive and they should fit together to form an attractive whole. Your body, your clothes, the furniture in your apartment, the paintings on your wall, the carpets on your floor. The style of each part contributes to the style of the whole.

The same is true at work. Everything that people associate with you is a part of you. This is obvious enough in the case of your office or your desk. But it's also true of the *little* pieces, the little pieces that you give out and send off every day without thinking. These little pieces can be permanent—a letter, a business card, a report, a résumé, a memorandum. Or they can be ephemeral—a brief encounter in the hall, instructions to your secretary, a meeting with your boss. No matter how small or insignificant it may seem, each piece carries a message about you with it. Make sure the message says what you want it to say. If each piece is as stylish as you can make it, the whole will be stylish. Details make the man.

133

Presenting Yourself on Paper

Many people don't meet you first in person. They first make your acquaintance in writing: in letters, résumés, memoranda, and other forms of presenting yourself on paper. You want to appear as stylish on paper as you do in person.

It's most important, of course, to have a good writing style. A person who writes good, clean, lucid prose makes one kind of impression on a reader. A person who writes complicated, boring, even ungrammatical prose makes another kind of impression. You know what kind of impression you want to make.

But, as in many other aspects of style, form is almost as important as content. The way you present what you say is almost as important as the way you say it or what you say. Any business letter is improved by being well-typed on good stationery. Even the most modest work experience sounds more impressive in a well-designed résumé. Everyone—even the best writer—must continually work to improve the quality of his writing. But in this section we give you several ideas on how you can improve the *appearance* of your statements on paper.

Stationery

The first step is to pick the right paper.

You should always have your own stationery. That goes for both business and personal correspondence. Unfortunately, if you work for a large organization, you may be stuck with what's in the stockroom. If you do choose your own stationery—or if you have a hand in choosing the firm's stationery—remember the basic rules of style.

First, the simpler, the better. The paper used in all business stationery should be white, pure white. Avoid colors, obvious textures, or background designs of any kind. The paper should also be a generous size. Save the dainty stuff for love notes. The best size is the most common: typewriter paper. It's more efficient. You can get more words to the page. Anything smaller indicates that you don't have much to say or that what you have to say isn't important. Both impressions are undesirable.

The restrictions are not as rigid with personal stationery. The paper can be smaller. Textures and even very light colors are permissible. But once you've found a good paper for your business stationery, we suggest you stick with it. After all, your friends have as much right to be impressed as your clients.

Once you've chosen the right paper, think about what goes on it. Printed at the top should be your first name, middle initial (your full middle name only if you use it), and last name. Never use just your last name, your initials, or other abbreviations. Addresses and telephone numbers are mandatory for business stationery, optional for personal stationery. Putting them on personal stationery may save you typing them repeatedly. But if you change addresses frequently, you'll end up throwing out a lot of expensive, unused stationery.

Your name and address should be printed modestly. The type face should be small enough that it doesn't dwarf the writing in the body of the letter. It should also be simple. Times roman or helvetica is fine. Italic or anything else is not. The printing should be black or gray: no colors, not even conservative ones like dark blue. For business stationery, a company emblem or logo is acceptable, but keep it small and, again, avoid colors, especially bright ones.

This may sound dull and unimpressive, but it's just the opposite. If you want stationery that's out of the ordinary, you don't have to achieve it with garish colors or snazzy lettering. Just specify a particularly thick stock of paper and have the letters embossed rather than printed. The elegance won't shout at the reader, of course. It wouldn't be real elegance if it did. But the reader will *feel* it the moment he opens the envelope and unfolds the paper. True elegance is always subtle.

Business Cards

You may have the same problem choosing business cards that you have choosing stationery: the choice may not be yours. Your firm or business may have a standard card, in which case you may only get to choose your personal card.

But whenever the choice is yours, we recommend that your card follow the same design as your stationery. It should be thick, white card stock, the same shade of white as your stationery. The color, ink, and type face should also match. Observe the same rules: no colors, no elaborate designs, no italics or clever quotations. Careful coordination is the key to a good personal design package.

In a business encounter, your card is your introduction. Put it to work for you. If your client needs your address and phone number, don't write it out every time; let the card provide the information. If you prefer being called by a nickname, let the card give your full name. If your name has an unusual spelling—Naifeh, rather than Smith, for example—let the card save you the trouble of conducting a spelling lesson. If your title is long and not very impressive (Assistant Deputy Curator of Decorative Arts at the Metropolitan Museum), let the card give the details (introduce yourself as a curator at the Met). In short, this small card can perform many awkward and time-consuming jobs. If you choose it carefully, it will perform them with style.

Writing a Business Letter

In business letters, as in most things, form is almost as important as content. How it *looks* makes almost as big an impression as what it *says*. We are not necessarily condoning this state of the art, merely describing it.

So how do you dress your letters to make the right impression? Begin with the stationery. Then get a good typist to type it for you on a good typewriter. Here are a few guidelines for you to follow.

1. Start with the return address and, if you think there's a chance the reader may want to contact you by telephone, your number as well. The date, unabbreviated, follows.

2. The next item is the address of the addressee. Use the person's *full* title and address. The more lines the address occupies, the more flattered the addressee will be.

3. Don't indent the name of the addressee. In fact, don't indent any of the paragraphs in the letter. It's much better form to separate the paragraphs by skipping a line between them.

If you're writing to a woman, use the title "Ms." unless you know to a certainty that she prefers "Miss," "Mrs.," or "Dr." If you don't know the person to whom you're writing, avoid sexist salutations ("Dear Sir," "Gentlemen," and the like). Stick with the more awkward but politically aware "To Whom It May Concern." When the person's name leaves some doubt as to his or her sex, *don't* guess. Omit the title altogether and use the full name: "Dear Merle Hartzler."

4. The only closing to use is "Sincerely." The rest are too complicated or too intimate. If the letter is to a friend, of course, you can be more personal.

5. Type your full name (first name, middle initial, and last name) several lines after the closing.

6. The last touch, and probably the most important, since it provides the only opportunity for individuality, is your signature. An impressive signature, one that's authoritative yet flowing, is impressive indeed. Spend the time to cultivate one. It's worth it. It should be legible, of course, but there's no reason it can't have an artistic quality to it.

Be sure to sign your full name every time, unless the letter is personal. Save your initials for office memoranda.

Writing a Résumé

Your résumé is your stand-in. It's there when you're not, often at times when you would most want to be present in person. It's there when people are considering whether or not to hire you, promote you, or award you some honor. It's there when salaries are being discussed, when you're being compared to someone else or sized up among a field of candidates.

Of course, you may already have had a chance to speak up for yourself at an interview. But when most of the decisions are actually being made, only your résumé is there to speak for you, to remind people of your assets long after they've forgotten what you look like or how you act. Be sure that your résumé makes as good an impression when you're gone as you did in person.

There are two basic rules in writing a résumé: First, keep it short and clear. Time is money. An employer with a hundred applications to read doesn't have time to dawdle over a long and chatty self-portrait. He won't be patient enough to *search* for the information he wants, either. The shorter and clearer your résumé is, the easier it will be for him to find what you want him to find and remember what you want him to remember. It also proves that you can prepare cohesive reports and memoranda, an important asset in any business.

Second, make the résumé fit the job. Let an interviewer know exactly what kind of job you want. Then tell him you have precisely the background needed to perform the job well. Tailor each element of your résumé to suit the task at hand. If you're applying for more than one kind of job, you may have to write more than one résumé.

Here are the areas your résumé should cover and a few rules for each.

Job Objective.   A lot of job hunting is shooting in the dark. You don't always know exactly what you're looking for; you just hope you'll find it. Your résumé should give the people who read it some idea of what you're looking for. If the job is undefined, or if the firm has more than one job you qualify for, they'll have some clue about how you'll fit in.

Of course, the problem is that often *you* don't know what you're looking for. That makes it hard to tell *them*. The best most of us can do is to relate our interests—writing, research, sales, public relations —and say we'd like a job that lets us pursue those interests somehow. You decide the *kind* of work you want to do; let the firm decide the specific job that's right for you.

There are other ways to use a résumé in which you don't need to list a job objective. If you're invited to give a lecture or you submit an article to a magazine, for example, your résumé is just a way of letting people know something about you. If you're applying for a specific position, a detailed description of the kind of work you want is superfluous. But even then, the trouble you take to make the résumé fit the situation will always be rewarded.

Personal. Include your address and telephone number (office and home). If an employer is interested in you, he'll want to contact you. And he won't want to hunt through your résumé to find out how. Whatever you do, don't count on the fact that he's saved your envelope or cover letter for the return address.

A birth date is also useful; it lets the employer know how old you are without computing your age from the date of your college graduation. However, if you'd rather have him forget your age—if he might think you're too young (or too old) for the job—leave it out. Let him ask about it after he's expressed an interest. It might not make so much difference at that point.

What about your height, weight, and other personal data? Leave it out. It's as simple as that. The color of your eyes shouldn't matter to your future employer.

Employment Experience. Start with the job you're in now, or your most recent job if you're not working at the moment. Then work back to your first job. Not too far; there's no need to include childhood paper routes.

There are two reasons for putting your job history in reverse chronological order. First, your most recent job is most relevant to your next job. If you're applying to be an insurance agent, the employer is more interested in knowing about your experience as a salesman for a large commercial firm than about your job as a checkout boy at the local grocery during high school. But there is another good reason. Your most recent job is also probably your most impressive one. And in writing a résumé, it's always a good idea to give them your best right up front. Remember it's a sales pitch, not "This Is Your Life."

List the title of your job first. Give it the most impressive sound you can without misrepresenting it. Just remember that sooner or later you'll have to explain it in detail.

If any of your jobs were part time, don't bother to say "full time" or "part time" before each job. Just place an asterisk after each part-time job entry, and define the asterisk as meaning "part time" at the end of the employment section.

Education.   List the school with its address, then the program and degree you received, and the date you received it. Again, as in the case of your employment, list your education in reverse chronological order. The last school on the list should be your high school. No one cares where you went to grade school.

Honors and Awards.   The bigger this section the better. Stretch it as far as your record (and your conscience) allow. If a prize or honor is not self-explanatory, give it a brief parenthetical explanation: "Dana Prize (for scholarship and athletic ability)." As a rule, you should leave out high school honors and awards.

Projects and Publications.   The importance of this section will vary depending on the kind of job you're applying for. A graphic designer needs to list all his major accomplishments; so does a writer. Include all books and magazine articles published to date.

Activities.   List all organizations or activities in which you are active as long as they are directly or indirectly relevant to your job. What do we mean by "indirectly"? If you want a job as a salesman, your Elks Club membership is indirectly related to your job. It says that you enjoy being with people—an important part of being a good salesman. If the activity is completely unrelated to your job, think twice before including it.

Also, no hobbies, no quotes, no anecdotes, no jokes.

References. Just say "References on request." Never include the names of references. Just a name, no matter how dazzling, will never get you very far.

Besides, if you're sending out a number of résumés, you may be subjecting that dazzling name to a bombardment of requests, many from employers you may not be very interested in. A good reference is an invaluable resource. Don't squander it on every passing job opportunity. You want all requests for references to come through you. That way you can direct the good job possibilities to your best references, protect your references from overuse, and keep in touch with them so that they're up to date.

Another don't: Don't give people as references simply because they have name value. Choose your references on the basis of how well they know you and how well they write, not how important they are. Nothing is less impressive than a letter of recommendation filled with generalizations and strings of adjectives written by someone who barely knows—or barely remembers—the person he's writing about. In particular, avoid letters from your Congressman that say you're a "fine, upstanding citizen."

Résumé Form. Once you've drafted your résumé, make sure it *looks* as good as it reads. Unless you have a very good typewriter— an IBM Selectric, in other words—spend the few dollars it costs to have it typed by a professional typist. Once it's typed, don't photo-copy it. Have it photostated. When you're reproducing many copies of a few pages, it's only slightly more expensive than photocopying and looks much, much better. One final word, in case we haven't already been clear enough: *white* paper, *black* ink, *simple* typeface. Nothing else.

Presenting Yourself in Person

These days, most business is transacted at a distance: over the phone, through the mails, by memoranda. It's fast, easy, direct, and impersonal. But don't be fooled. Almost all *important* business is still transacted in person. The man with presence, the man with a warm, aggressive, engaging *personal* manner still has an edge. So remember, no matter how well you write, no matter how well you present yourself on paper, sooner or later—probably when the occasion is most important—you're going to have to show your face.

Who would consider hiring someone, especially for an important position, sight unseen? If you're employing a consultant, you want to meet him first. If you're contemplating a business deal, you want to meet your prospective partner. The first thing any lawyer wants to do before taking a case is meet the client, and the first thing any client wants to do is meet his lawyer.

Why do you think law firms and corporations spend hundreds of thousands of dollars each year sending recruiters to the top law schools and business schools? Although grades and recommendations are important, they believe there's still nothing quite as reliable or informative as a face-to-face assessment. You may find it consoling or you may find it old-fashioned. But those firms and corporations are probably right.

The Interview

Most people think of interviews as rare events. And they're glad of it. They remember when they graduated from school and interviewed for their first job: the trauma, the disappointment. Never again, they vow.

In fact, most people have interviews every day of their lives. Whenever there's a meeting, there's an interview. Whenever two people "get a look at each other," there's an interview. Whenever you dine out with a date, have lunch with a colleague, talk to your secretary, or visit a friend, you're conducting an interview.

The only difference between these everyday situations and job interviews is that the stakes are not so high. Of course, interviews also have different purposes. With your colleagues and secretaries, you have *information* interviews. The purpose is to trade information that you already have and maybe generate a little new information. With a date, you probably have an *assessment* interview. You're sizing each other up. Job interviews are basically assessment interviews.

Finally, there are *adversary* interviews. These were invented by lawyers primarily for use in the courtroom. Unfortunately, their popularity has spread. Most people make the mistake of thinking that job interviews are adversary interviews when, in fact, only *bad* job interviews are adversary interviews.

You can learn a lot from thinking of the job interview as an assessment interview: a kind of "date" where you and the interviewer can size each other up. After all, the question is the same: What are the chances of making a successful relationship together? To answer the question correctly, you need to know something about each other.

Just as you wouldn't pick a woman at random out of the phone book and ask her out to dinner, don't interview with random employers. Have a sense of what you're looking for.

If you send your résumé and the employer asks for an interview, at least you know he's interested. Take it for the good sign that it is. Respond by showing you're interested, too. The best way to do that is to *prepare* for the interview in advance.

Advance Preparation

If you've got a date, it helps to know whether the woman likes surprises or dislikes wine, whether she adores roses or abhors disco. If you care about her, you'll probably go to the trouble of finding out as much as you can. You should do the same for an interview.

Research the job. Learn as much as you can about the firm and the kind of work it does. You'll ask better questions, seem more professional, appear more interested, and exude more self-confidence.

Don't forget to prepare your body too. (We won't mention the romantic parallels here.) Get a good night's sleep. If the interview is in another city, don't get up with the farmers and watch the sunrise from an airplane window. Arrive the night before and stay in a hotel. No matter where an interview is, get there at least ten minutes ahead of time. Some people play it really safe by arriving an hour early, then getting something to eat in a nearby coffee shop. That may seem excessive, but at least they're spared the anxiety of slow taxi rides through unexpected traffic jams. Besides, a little time without the worry of being late will give you a chance to collect your thoughts—and your self-confidence. Better yet, use the time to check the firm out. Walk around, talk to people, assess the mood of the place.

Another good idea if you arrive early: Talk to the interviewer's secretary. Everyone enjoys a little attention. A few pleasant words, a few sincere questions can win you an important ally. Chances are, she'll find a time to tell the interviewer *her* favorite. If he respects her opinions—which he probably does—you've got an edge.

Conversation with the secretary is not just a polite gesture. You can probably learn a lot more about the firm from her than from a formal interview. Remember, this is an *assessment* interview. You and the employer are getting a look at *each other*. In your nervousness, don't forget that you should be assessing *him*, too. After all, finding out whether the job is right for you is as important as finding out whether you are right for the job.

What to Wear to an Interview

What do you wear to an interview? It depends on the job you're interviewing for. If it's a lifeguard job, a business suit is probably unnecessary. If it's an executive position in a large firm, a swimsuit would be inappropriate. The best tactic is to wear what people already *in* the organization wear. Follow suit (so to speak). If there is some doubt, if a reconnaissance of the offices turns up both dark pinstripes *and* leisure suits, play it safe and be conservative. Always err on the side of restraint.

Of course, if no one in the firm ever wears a jacket of any kind, you don't want to show up in a three-piece suit. On the other hand, if everyone in the firm wears three-piece suits, you don't want to show up in a sports jacket or, even worse, shirt sleeves. This is where a little advance knowledge of the firm can really pay off.

One rule holds whatever the job: Get a good hair-cut, and shave just before you go to the interview.

Stating Your Case

We said an interview is like a date. *Both* are a little like a wrestling match. It's important to assert your strength right from the beginning. Be polite, but be assertive. Show your respect by speaking in polite phrases. Use a deferential title: "sir" or "ma'am." But stay in control of the conversation. Ask incisive questions. Unless you're unusually quick, you'd better think them up in advance. Direct the conversation toward your strengths and away from your weaknesses. Don't bully and don't dodge, but keep it positive. If you *sound* convinced that you're right for the job, you stand a better chance of convincing the interviewer.

What questions should you ask? Ask about the firm, about the kind of work you'd be doing. Try to frame the basic questions in interesting ways. Ask what a typical day would be like. Ask what you might find in your in-basket the day you begin. Ask whether you'll have the opportunity to do some creative work. Obviously, the questions will depend on the nature of the job. An accountant might want to know about the pension plan, a stuntman about the disability benefits.

Whatever you do, don't ask about things you should already know: pay, hours, working conditions, and so on. Even if asking is the only way to find out, don't ask. Let the interviewer tell you. It should at least *appear* that you're interested in the work, not the pay.

Demonstrate your enthusiasm. If you can't demonstrate it, *fake* it. A job interview is not the place to be cool. Most firms are looking for aggressive, ambitious people who want to work hard and advance within the firm and are willing to devote several decades to the effort. But don't worry if you don't fit this description. Very few people do, certainly not enough to fill all the available positions.

On the other hand, don't let your enthusiasm get the upper hand. You don't want the interviewer to think he's got the only crap game in town, even if he does. Make it clear that it's just as important for *him* to sell the job as it is for *you* to sell yourself. Employers, like lovers, will find you more attractive if your enthusiasm is edged with at least a little disinterest. In fact, take a tip from love relations by interposing a jealousy object. Let the interviewer know—subtly, of course—that you're looking at other positions.

The point is this: In an interview, as in a date, you have to play the role your interviewer (or your partner) expects. It's part of the game. If the game goes well—if you get the job, or win the girl—you can drop the role and be yourself again. Just be sure that when the game's over you still want the prize.

A few final words of advice. Don't worry if the interviewer begins to question you closely. At least you've sparked his interest. He may in fact be testing to see how you function under fire. An *intense interviewer* is almost always a good sign. A bad sign is when the interviewer looks drowsy.

The Other Side of the Desk

Finally, a few words for the *interviewer*. The interview is no place for bad manners—on *either* side of the desk. Being an interviewer doesn't give you a license to embarrass, scold, hound, or abuse people. If anything, because it's usually conducted with a stranger, an interview should be a showcase of politeness and consideration.

That doesn't mean you can't ask hard questions. Just make sure they're relevant to the job you're discussing. For example: Why is a candidate from the East Coast looking at jobs in California? This is a reasonable question, but there are many unreasonable ways to ask it. While it's all right to ask someone why he's interviewing in your area of the country, it would be impolite to ask, "Do you want this job just because you like our climate?" Accusatory questions like this are an affront. A self-respecting candidate should tell you he's offended by them.

Avoid cute questions. Committees for the Rhodes Scholarship, for example, are notorious for their banal inquiries. "How do you get along with your mother?" or "Which would you rather be, an apple or an anvil?" This kind of amateur psychoanalysis is an insult to an earnest candidate. It's also unfair: The person who asks the question seldom knows how to interpret the answer.

As a rule, the best way to get to know a person, whether it's an interview or not, is to make him feel *comfortable*. Most people don't respond with candor to insults, challenges, tricky questions, accusations, or misguided efforts at psychoanalysis. Try being friendly instead. Spend the first few minutes of the interview putting the other person at ease. Ask some easy questions. Find a topic that interests him and let him talk about it for a while. Remember, the idea is to find out as much as you can about him. Put him at ease and you *will* find out. Put him on his guard and the interview will be a struggle.

One final point. You're not the only one who will be leaving the interview with impressions. If he's a good candidate, his impression of *you* will be as important as your impression of *him*. If you later give him an offer, he'll remember the interview, and it may have a lot to do with his decision to take the job or not. As in love, if you play *too* hard to get you'll wind up with nothing.

Getting Along at the Office

Even if you manage to perfect your stationery, your résumé, and your interviewing technique, there's still more to style. We've argued all

along that style is not just what you wear or how you look. Style is
not just appearance; it's *attitude*. You can dress yourself in the finest
clothes, collect the finest art, appoint your home and your office
impeccably. But if you treat people boorishly, you're still a boor—an
attractive, well-dressed, erudite boor.

Manners are the soul of style. By manners, we don't just mean
the do's and don'ts of Emily Post. We mean the rules of behavior
that require fairness, honesty, and decency in all your dealings. The
next few sections concern some of these basic good manners and how
they can be applied in the office—whether you're dealing with your
boss, your secretary, or your colleagues. Follow these simple steps
and they'll do more for your style than a rack of fine clothes.

You might think these steps are manipulative. Well, they are and
they aren't. True, they'll help you in your career. But we're not saying that stylish good manners will help your career more than calcu-
lated ruthlessness. In fact, most books on success recommend the
latter for getting ahead. What we *are* saying is that there's a right
way and a wrong way to be successful, just as there's a right way and
a wrong way to decorate your home. In both cases, the right way is
the stylish way. This is not a book on ethics, but we can't help noting
that decency and morality, like simplicity and authenticity, are always in style.

Intimacy or Deference: The Delicate Balance

In most other countries, a chain of command is clear and rigid. You
know your superiors, your subordinates, and your place between
them. Relationships up and down the ladder are *always* formal. You
bow to your employer; your employees bow to you. Your title is
always used.

In America, on the other hand, we're concerned with maintaining
at least the appearance of democracy, Whereas *deference* is the rule
in most offices around the world, *intimacy,* or at least the *pretense*
of intimacy, is the rule in this country. You would never think of
bowing to the president of your company or saluting your boss.

Everybody is supposed to be called by his first name or, better yet, by his nickname. Even the president of the United States is supposed to be a regular guy.

But if there were no deference, there'd be no authority. If American offices *really* operated on the basis of intimacy, decisions would have to be made by consensus. The fact is, they don't and they aren't. Sooner or later, when a decision has to be made, somebody has to make it. And his decision is law, whether his "friends" in the office like it or not.

That's why professional and personal relationships don't mix. In a personal relationship, you can't stop being friends. In a professional relationship, there are times when you *have* to stop being friends.

The problem of striking the right balance between deference and intimacy comes up in many ways. For example, what do you call your boss (to his face, that is)? Do you call him by his last name? His first name? "Sir," "Mr. Smith?" You want to be respectful without being servile, friendly, but not fatuous.

Your safest bet is to begin formally. Warm up only if your boss asks you to. Call him "sir" or "Mr. Smith." If he corrects you, continue to call him "sir" until he corrects you again. If he corrects you a third time, chances are he really *does* want you to call him by his first name. Whatever you do, don't assume that all bosses *really* want to be called by their first names or nicknames. Perhaps your boss's first name is "Farquar," or his nickname is "Twinkles." You should soon be able to sense the kind of relationship he wants to establish. Until you do, stay distant and deferential.

Ignore those visions of quick promotions and favored treatment. As we said, it's almost impossible to maintain a *professional* relationship and a *personal* relationship with the same person. Sooner or later, the same friendship that wins you favors is going to earn you grudges, certainly from your colleagues, maybe even from your boss. It's best to keep your distance—politely but firmly.

The same holds true for your relationships with your subordinates. Always keep a little distance. Being their boss is a full-time job. Let someone else be their best friend. If nothing else, it will make difficult decisions like promoting and firing much easier. The distance will also make it easier to win and maintain their respect. We're not recommending that you be pompous or aloof, of course, just that you limit your role in their lives. After all, they're business colleagues, not relatives.

Finally, remember that *consideration* is an important part of *deference*. You should never upstage your boss. If you went to a more prestigious school than he did, don't talk about schools. If you dress better than he does, don't talk about clothes. If he's depressed, don't tell him about the marvelous weekend you just enjoyed. You would certainly want the same consideration from *your* employees.

Not Too Close

If you keep a safe distance from your boss and from your subordinates, must you do the same with your other colleagues? As a rule, yes, and for the same reasons. They may be friends and "equals," but they can also be competitors. In most firms, your success is your colleagues' failure. If you win a promotion, they don't. When a position becomes available and you must vie for it with your "friends," what becomes of the friendship? You may feel compelled to act in ways, or you may be treated in ways, that are not exactly friendly.

The only fair and decent way to maintain a professional relationship is to make it clear from the start that it's a professional relationship and not a personal one. And the only way to do that is to keep your distance. Not far, but far enough so that your colleagues understand that you feel no personal obligation. Competing with colleagues is not unfair. Competing with friends *is*. The only inexcusable breach of good manners is to *play* the part of a personal friend, then treat your friends professionally when the competitive heat is on.

Needless to say, the same logic argues against office romances. Work and love are a bad mix. Try them together and neither will turn out well. You'll see too much of each other, talk too much about work, upset whatever working relationship you may have had, and make ending the relationship impossibly awkward. At the ten o'clock coffee break you'll be facing the woman you broke up with last night. Save yourself the monumental embarrassment of dictating a letter to someone who just rejected you. Leave your affairs or your wife, or both, at home.

Share the Credit

It's simple courtesy to give credit where credit is due. It's both courteous and *politic* sometimes to give credit where it is not due, or at least to give more credit than is due. In most businesses, you rarely get the chance to do real solo work. Writing a report isn't like writing a novel. Chances are, someone gave you the idea or at least the assignment, someone helped you in your thinking, someone read your draft, and someone typed it. These are all debts you should acknowledge.

It's always good to give your superiors some of the credit for your successes. It's good manners and good politics. Never crow about a project you're proud of without noting your boss's contribution. If he didn't make a contribution, acknowledge it anyway. It's a good bet that he had *some* part in getting you the project. Spread your gratitude around and you'll make friends instead of enemies. Your accomplishments will win your boss's respect and confidence, instead of his envy and suspicion. People will always know who *really* did the work.

The same is true of your secretary. A good secretary can double the amount of usable working time you have. Even if she never contributes an idea, she makes it possible for you to think. Acknowledge that, not just to her, but to her colleagues, your colleagues, and anybody else who will listen. Your secretary probably already knows that her work is essential. But it will help her morale to know that *you* think it's essential. Concern for morale is good office policy. Concern for other people's feelings is just good manners.

Some Suggestions

Avoid Office Gossip. Again, it's simply bad manners to talk about people when they're not around to defend themselves. The trouble is, gossip is what most conversation consists of. Most of us would like to think we prefer to talk about the really important issues in life: philosophy, religion, ethics. But most of the time, what we really like to talk about is each other. That doesn't make it right, however.

Gossip can also get you into trouble. You may think your listener has a closed mouth. But it usually doesn't take very long for whatever you've said to reach the ears of the person you said it about. *Indulging* in gossip makes you more *vulnerable* to gossip. So if you feel a need to relate the latest foibles of the people who work in your office, do it at home, not at the office.

Keep Your Confidences. When you tell somebody you'll keep something secret, keep it secret. This is a common courtesy known as not lying. Don't just preface each retelling of the secret with a line such as, "Do you promise not to tell anyone?" If you promise not to tell anyone, *don't tell anyone.* If you can't resist telling secrets, either refuse to hear them or warn the person from the start. Unfortunately, it's difficult to look at your boss and tell him he can't talk to you confidentially because you know you'll blab everything. So try a different approach. Instead of not listening to secrets, try not telling them.

If you can tame the urge to tell secrets, you'll quickly win the trust and confidence of your superiors as well as your subordinates. A man who keeps confidences is rare indeed. At first people may dislike you for being closed-mouthed. They may think it's a sign of unfriendliness. But in time they'll grow to respect you for it.

Keep the Office in Perspective. For many people, work is life. At home, at the office, in between, it doesn't matter where, it's all work. Gone before sunrise, back past sunset, with a briefcase full of papers to fill the gap. Workaholism, like alcoholism, is widespread, growing fast, and often fatal.

Of course, there's nothing wrong with enjoying your work. Who doesn't want a job he can enjoy? Hell holds no fate worse than getting up in the morning and dreading the day ahead—watching the clock, stretching coffee breaks, longing for the weekend as if you were a child again and Saturday were Christmas. How much better it is to like your work for the *work* and not for the paycheck.

But no matter how much you enjoy your work, keep it in perspective. Balance is as important in your outlook as it is on your walls. You know you've *lost* your perspective when you can't enjoy a vacation because the details of the project you left behind keep running through your mind, or you feel lost without the phone ringing in your ears. Signs like these should make you stop and think. Are you neglecting the rest of your life: the arts, travel, emotional relationships?

The problem is even more urgent if you have a family or an important relationship. In that case you're not only cheating yourself; you're cheating others *and* cheating yourself.

If He Is a She

What if your boss is a *woman*? The chances of such a fate are getting better and better, so it's a good idea to give it some thought. For the most part, deal with her the same way you would deal with a male. Of course, there are some obvious differences. Don't call her "sir." Don't offer her cigars (unless you've seen her smoke them). Don't share your sexual exploits. Don't refer to her "wife." Don't whistle and don't pinch. But there are also some subtler guidelines you should be aware of.

First, demonstrate your respect for women professionals. If you don't have any, develop some in a hurry. Alas, sexist jokes are out, even in jest. Mind your chauvinism. You can let her walk through a door first because you'd probably do that for a male employer. But don't hold her chair unless she appears to expect it. This isn't manipulation; it's good manners.

Finally, whatever you do, give the relationship a chance. Don't decide from the very start that you simply *can't* work with a woman, because chances are good that you *can*. Like many men who are confident of their masculinity, you may even find that you like working for a woman more than working for a man. It's a novel situation, and as in most novel situations, people try a little harder to make it work.

For More Information

Michael Korda, *Power: How to Get It, How to Use it* (New York: Random House, 1975).
Michael Korda, *Success* (New York, Random House, 1977).
Jean Reed, ed., *Résumés that Get Jobs* (New York: Arco, 1963).

PART FIVE:

At Leisure

CHAPTER NINE:

Filling the Spare Hours

Filling the Spare Hours in Style

No matter how much time you spend at the office, on vacation, or out on the town, sooner or later you have to come home. Unless you're married or permanently attached, sooner or later you'll be alone—with time on your hands.

These are the spare hours. Just because we call them spare doesn't mean we think you can do without them. How you fill these hours is an important part of being an interesting, stylish person. After all, it's your spare-time activities that lend color to your conversation, variety to your work, and interest to your life.

We've already mentioned several activities that can fill your spare hours in style: Exercising, for example, or buying art. In this chapter we'll add a few more.

The *most* stylish way to spend your time alone is to be creative. Write a novel, or at least some poetry. If you have the training, compose some music. Play an instrument. Sing in a choir. Try your hand at painting or sculpture. Build furniture. Design houses. As long as you enjoy the activity it doesn't matter how good you are.

If you haven't got the time, training, or patience to make these artistic activities satisfying, try something a little less ambitious. *Read* a book. *Listen* to some music. Visit the local galleries. Take photographs. We've included some helpful hints on how to start a record collection.

If you're like many Americans, your creative urge may take a more materialistic form. You may prefer to look at, read about, or listen to things you can buy. You may prefer to spend your spare hours in a shopping mall rather than an art museum. If so, you'll also find sections on three of the most stylish consumer items: cars, cameras, and stereo systems. If you do it right, each one can be as much fun to buy as it is to own.

As we said, it's always more stylish to invent your own toys than it is to buy them. But whether you invent them or buy them, stylish toys—stylish *activities*—will make the most of your spare hours.

The Automobile

There was a time when a car was more than just a means of transportation. It was a symbol. For a man, it meant freedom and masculinity. Cars were the mating feathers of a technological society with more Freudian overtones than a cigar.

Today, things have changed. The emphasis is now on function, not fantasy. A man with a powerful way of dealing with people is now more impressive than a man with a powerful car. Cars are getting back to basics—to getting people from one place to another, cheaply, quickly, efficiently.

The change has a lot to do with ecology. It's *stylish* today to worry about the environment. When we see a man driving a big car today, we don't admire him for his wealth. We condemn him for squandering all that gas and polluting the air. A high mileage rate has replaced car size as the most respected status symbol.

If less is more, then maybe the most stylish thing is not to own a car at all. And, in fact, if you live in a large city with no parking, heavy traffic, bad roads, and good public transportation, you're probably better off without one. The few times you need a car—when you go on a trip that's too long for a cab or bus and too short for a plane—rent one. Rental rates are high, but just compare them to the cost of buying, maintaining, and insuring your own car. Economy—the sensible variety, not stinginess—is always fashionable.

Yet most people still insist on owning their own cars. So the question is, how do you select one? As in all other matters of style, ask yourself what the car *says* about you, what kind of image it conveys. A stylish car *looks* good, of course. But it isn't just a matter of esthetics. It's also a matter of practicality.

Practicality and Esthetics

It's *stylish* to have the right car for your own special needs. Do you want quick transportation or plenty of room? Do you want a car in order to go skiing in Vermont or to ferry clients from store to store? Maybe what you really want isn't transportation at all. Maybe what you want is a hobby—something to occupy your weekends. Each need demands a different solution. The stylish solution is always the one that satisfies the need.

So, in choosing a car, think first about practical matters: cost, mileage rates, quality of construction, ease of repair, comfort, and safety. If you want help, consult *Consumer Reports*. Or find the annual issue of *Road and Track* magazine in which the editors pick the best cars in each of ten categories, based on model and price. Whether you're looking for a middle-priced luxury sedan or a sports car for under $6,000, here's the place to start your search.

As for *esthetics*, follow the old rule: the simpler the better. Look for the cleanest lines you can find. Then, once you've found them, don't spoil them. Preserve the beauty of a simple design and avoid the extra expense by omitting flashy options. Practical ones are acceptable: power steering, automatic transmission, air conditioning for hot climates, even a sun roof or a cassette recorder. But be careful not to turn a good thing bad. If you add too many decorative options, you can ruin the good lines of even the best car.

For example, many cars come in "custom" two-toned versions. The word "custom" is designed to make you think it's an improvement. It's not. On cars—as on shoes—one color is enough.

Also:

No leatherette roofs.

No porthole side windows you can't see out of.

No racing stripes on cars that don't race.

No elaborate hub caps that only tempt thieves.

No crushed-velvet interiors.

No dice, religious figurines, or any other variety of dashboard decoration.

No decoration, period.

Color

The color you select, like the model you choose, depends on the use you plan to make of the car. If business clients or colleagues will ride in your car often, choose a conservative color. Dark blue, silver, or gray is best. Black is for hearses and limousines.

If your work and your car never intersect, something more cheerful is called for. Try lighter colors in unusual tonalities. Avoid hot pink.

Foreign versus American

Foreign cars are the new status symbols of the highway. As a rule, they're better built and better looking. Unfortunately, they're also more expensive and harder to repair. Try to find a fanbelt for your Fiat in Lander, Wyoming.

So if it's just style you're after, save your patriotism for the Fourth of July and buy foreign. This is especially true if you live in the city and seldom venture into the backwoods. On the other hand, if the nearest foreign car dealer or mechanic is somewhere over the mountains, save your style for the closet and stick with Detroit.

Recommended Cars

For style, nothing matches the Mercedes-Benz. They're so common among high-level executives that they're almost a condition of employment. If you have pangs of conscience, economy, or ecology about owning a Mercedes, buy a diesel. Better yet, buy a used one. People will think you anticipated the rush.

The Rolls-Royce is as attractive as the Mercedes but extremely expensive, even by luxury car standards. Of course, if you can afford it, the Rolls *is* the best car in the world and worth every penny of its house-sized price tag.

If, by some freak chance, you don't find the Mercedes attractive, try a BMW or a Jaguar. They're equally stylish and a little cheaper. If you want something snappier (and if you don't need to be conservative), try a Porsche. Somewhat more sedate but still acceptable is the Volvo.

But remember, there's no need to spend $20,000 on a car. An expensive car can be stylish, but it's just as stylish to do without one. Why not buy a cheaper car and spend the savings on something more permanent (like a painting), something more educational (like a trip to Europe), or something more worthwhile (like charity).

The classic cheap car is also German and has been for decades. The Volkswagen Rabbit—like its predecessor, the Bug—is tough, handsome, and economical. If you want to spend a little more, try the Volkswagen Scirocco or Honda Accord; a little less, the Honda CVCC.

If you want to buy American or the dollar sinks so far that you can't buy anything else, try the Chevrolet Malibu Classic, a solid, medium-priced sedan with excellent efficiency ratings and the best American design in memory.

For More Information

The current issue of *Consumer Guide* (New York: Publications International).

Cameras

We said that the most stylish way to fill your spare hours is to be creative: Paint a picture, compose some music, write a book. The problem is that most people don't have the training, the talent, or the time to be creative. Or at least they *think* they don't. Actually, there are many ways to be creative that don't require a great deal of artistic talent. Photography is one of them. You don't need to be a professional photographer or to spend days in the darkroom to take pictures creatively. All you need is the right equipment and a little practice.

A Good Dealer Is the Key

How do you buy the right camera? The same way you buy the right stereo or the right painting. Find a good dealer. Talk to him. Tell him the kind of pictures you want to take and how much you want to spend. A good dealer will give you good advice. After all, he wants you to come back. To find a good dealer, ask friends, photographers, or dealers in photographs—anyone who knows something about cameras.

But in order to get the most out of a good dealer, you have to know enough to ask the right questions. Here's what you need to know.

What You Don't Want

First things first. Before we talk about the cameras you *want*, let's talk about the cameras you *don't* want. Instamatics, for example. You don't want instamatics because they don't take good pictures. Sure, they're easy to load and easy to shoot, but, as you'll see, so are some good 35 mm cameras. The reason that instamatics can't take good pictures is that they can't use 35 mm film. The negatives are too small and cramped to produce anything but a blurred picture. If a blurred picture is good enough for you, it shouldn't be—or you shouldn't be taking pictures.

The same is true of Polaroid cameras. It's quite a technological achievement to be able to see a photograph the minute you take it. But it's not a photographic achievement. If you buy a Polaroid, buy it for the novelty value, not for the quality of the prints. A Polaroid is great at a party. You can show everyone a picture and get a good warm laugh. You can even put the picture in your scrapbook and get the same warm laugh year after year. But if you want great pictures, not just great memories, get a better camera.

What You Want

There are two basic kinds of cameras: rangefinder cameras and single-lens reflex cameras. The kind of camera you want obviously depends on the kind of pictures you want to take.

Rangefinder Cameras. If you're more interested in taking an occasional good picture than in becoming a professional photographer—if you want something easy to use, easy to carry, and easy to afford—then what you want is a rangefinder camera.

Rangefinders are a lot like instamatics. They come in one piece, so there are no removable lenses to worry about. Many are also fully automatic, so there are no light settings or exposure times to complicate things. Of course, the more *automatic* they are, the more *expensive* they are. Some people also prefer nonautomatic cameras for the same reason some people prefer nonautomatic cars: They give you more control.

The cheapest good-quality fully automatic camera is the Canonet 28 for under $100. But if you want the highest quality for the lowest price, the best deal in rangefinders is the Canon GIII for about $150. It loads like an instamatic: Just open the back and drop in the film. And it's almost impossible to take a bad picture. The camera chooses the right light exposure automatically. If there isn't enough light in the room, the camera won't click. But if you want to do things yourself, the Canon GIII has the advantage of operating as a nonautomatic camera as well.

If it's the size you like about instamatics, there are several good rangefinders to choose from, the Minox 35 EL, for example. It's fully automatic and about the size of a cigarette pack. Designed in Germany, the Minox is also handsome, simple, and sleek in the best Bauhaus tradition. The price is about $200.

Single-Lens Reflex Camera.   If you want good pictures, flexibility, and control, and you don't mind the effort and expense necessary to have them, buy a single-lens reflex camera. The main advantage, of course, is interchangeable lenses. They allow you to make the most of each picture. But a word of warning. The only reason to buy a single-lens reflex camera is if you want to be creative in your photography. If all you really want is an impressive camera case loaded with lenses, forget it. Buy a rangefinder instead.

The single-lens reflex camera to buy is a Nikon. The manufacturer calls it "The professionals' choice." This is *one* advertising claim that isn't an empty boast. The other good brands are also Japanese: Canon, Pentax, Minolta. They run about $100 cheaper than the equivalent Nikon. But, if you can afford it, persevere and get a Nikon. The extra cost is worth it. A good camera is a lifetime investment, not a place to count pennies. Try the Nikon FM, about $350 with lens. Or, if you want an automatic camera, the Nikon FE at about $450.

These days, most lenses are designed by computer, so one lens is basically as good as another. Be wary of price differences based on claims of lens superiority. A 50 mm lens has long been considered the standard lens. But many photographers have recently begun to use 35 mm lenses instead. There's no real difference in *quality*. It's just that the experts feel the character of a picture taken with a 35 mm lens approaches more closely what the human eye actually sees. If you have a 50 mm lens and want a second lens, try a wide-angle 28 mm rather than a 35 mm lens.

Used Cameras

Looks are an important part of style. But so is economy. Used cameras may not look as good as the latest models, but when you compare prices you may find that, in this case at least, economy is the better part of style.

The problem is rising camera costs. Labor and material costs are up. The dollar is down. Japanese cameras—90 percent of all cameras are Japanese—grow more expensive by the month. That makes used cameras a better bargain each year. Besides, used older cameras are often better made than newer ones.

There's really no need to worry about the quality of used merchandise either. Inspect it yourself. Unless the lens is visibly scratched or is difficult to adjust, it's probably in good condition. If you harbor any doubts, most good-quality used cameras come with a warranty. If there isn't one, ask a camera repairman to check it out for you. Your skepticism will only cost about $10.

If you're looking for a used camera, you might as well look for the best. Here are a few great cameras that are *only* available used, with the prices you should expect to pay.

1. Canon FTB: $150
2. Nikormat: $250
3. Nikon F: $300

Dream Machines

Of course, there are better cameras than a Nikon. In the 35 mm category, there is the German Leica, which costs about a thousand dollars but is so well built that use will only increase its value. Beyond that are box cameras like the incomparable Hasselblad, the camera the astronauts took to the moon. But before entering these deep financial waters, you should decide whether it's a career in photography you want, or just a few good pictures.

How To Take Pictures

Now that you have your camera, how do you use it? Take a course. Learn from a friend. Or read Henry Horenstein's *Black and White Photography: A Basic Manual* (Boston: Little, Brown, 1974). It's a good guide to basic black-and-white photography and darkroom work. If you go to all the trouble and expense of acquiring a fine camera, you might as well learn how to use it properly.

For More Information

Norman Snyder, ed., *The Photography Catalog* (New York: Harper & Row, 1976).

Stereo

It's possible—indeed, *preferable*—to live without a television set. A stereo is another matter. Unless you don't care for music, a good stereo system is essential. And if you don't already like music, now's the time to start. As you'll see, it's not as expensive as you might think.

Actually, what keeps many people from acquiring a stereo isn't the expense. It's the confusion—all that talk of speakers, receivers, turntables, cartridges, and tape decks. True, buying a stereo system can be complicated, especially since the fashion is to buy separate components, not compact systems. But there's nothing about it you can't learn in a few short lessons and a few trips to your local stereo shop.

First, you should understand why you have to buy components separately, why you can't just walk into a store and buy a compact stereo system. The problem is that stereo components are not compatible. A tone arm needs to be very stable, yet speakers vibrate. Records need to keep cool to prevent warping, yet receivers generate heat. A stereo system generates stereo sound. A single speaker generates monaural sound. So the speakers need to be apart and away from the receiver which, in turn, needs to be away from the turntable. In case you haven't gotten the idea, don't settle for a compact system.

The Components

1. *The Turntable.* The turntable is the simplest component in the system. It does its job if it keeps the records quietly rotating at a constant speed. The lighter the tone arm, the better the turntable. A light "tracking" weight means the needle exerts the least amount of pressure on the record surface. The less pressure it exerts, the less wear there is on your records.

2. *The Cartridge.* You can't just buy a needle. It has to be attached to a *cartridge.* The quality of the needle is important. After all, it's the only thing that touches the surface of the record. But the cartridge has a lot more to do with the quality of the sound your system produces. It converts the bumps and grooves of the plastic into an electronic signal that can be processed into sound.

3. *The Receiver.* The receiver processes the electronic signals and sends them on to the speakers. Actually, a receiver is *three* components: a pre-amplifier, a power amplifier, and a tuner. A tuner is another name for a radio. Amplifiers and tuners can be purchased separately, but a single receiver is adequate for all but the most fanatic stereo buffs. For most people, separate amplifiers and tuners are more trouble than they're worth. They may give you more knobs to play with, but they also give you more wires, more interference, and more breakdowns.

4. *The Speakers.* Speakers take the processed signal from the receiver and convert it into sound—into the motion of air. Each speaker

box contains a set of different-sized cones, which vibrate, setting the air in musical motion around them. Not surprisingly, speakers have a lot to do with the quality of sound you hear from the system.

Additional Equipment

Other items can be added to a basic stereo system: tape decks, cassette recorders, head phones, pre-amps, quad adopters, and so on. The list of options is endless. Before you buy them, decide whether you really need them.

Tape and cassette machines are supposed to *save* you money. The idea is to tape other people's records, so you don't have to buy your own. Tapes are also easier to store, easier to use, easier to maintain, and, of course, reusable.

So much for the idea. In fact, new tapes and cassettes—especially good ones—are almost as expensive as the records they replace. And taping records is no thrill. Perhaps that's why statistics show that many people who own tape recorders rarely use them. So why not spend the $400 that a good tape deck costs on another eighty of your favorite records.

If you do want a tape deck, should you buy open reel or cassette? Cassettes are increasingly popular, mainly because of their efficiency (no tedious tape-threading). But despite the recent technological advances in cassette decks, open-reel tape decks continue to produce a better sound, though some experts think they are still not as good, by and large, as a turntable and records.

The best open-reel machines are made by Revox, but they'll add about $1,000 to $1,500 to the cost of your system. If the convenience of a cassette recorder is worth the loss of quality to you, try a Toshiba or Aiwa. Neither will set you back more than about $275.

The same goes for head phones. Some people prefer the sound of headphones to the sound of speakers. But the best reason to own headphones isn't sound; it's manners. Headphones allow you to enjoy your music without sharing it—an important plus if you share the same space but not the same musical tastes with someone.

Like all components, headphones come in a wide range of prices. The cheapest are *dynamic* headphones. You can get a pair of Pioneer SE 205 headphones, for example, for as little as $20. Better sounding, and more expensive, are *orthodynamic* headphones, such as the Yamaha HP 2s for $50. If your pocketbook is bulging, try STAX SR 44's at $90. And if you're insanely devoted to acoustic electronics, you can enjoy the STAX SRX3 for a mere $260.

Listen for Yourself

The best way to choose a stereo system is to listen and compare. Go to a good stereo shop, tell the salesperson what you want to pay, then listen to the various systems available in your price range. There won't be as much difference between the receivers, the turntables, and the cartridges, so pay especially close attention to the speakers.

Different speakers are better for different kinds of music. Be sure to get a speaker that suits your musical taste. A classical music buff will want an "accurate" speaker—one that reproduces sound exactly. A rock fan may want a little extra *umph* in the bass.

The best way to get what's right for your own taste is to take along a favorite record when you shop. That way you can listen to speakers playing the kind of music you want them for.

Choosing the Right Stereo Shop

The easiest mistake to make in choosing a stereo is to choose the wrong stereo shop, and it's a common mistake. The problem is that you really need both a good stereo *shop* and a good stereo *person*. Even the best shops are often manned by high-pressure salesmen who take advantage of your ignorance to sell you pet brands or high mark-up items instead of what's best for what you want to pay. If they work on commission—and most do—the salesmen may also try hard to jack up your price range. Beware of lines like, "If you were only willing to spend another hundred you could get twice the system."

Don't go to a large department store. You may find courtesy, but

you won't find expertise. The salesman was probably just switched
from ladies' shoes. You also won't find much selection. So stick to a
specialty stereo shop. Here are some things to look for:

1.   Good selection.
2.   Knowledgeable and helpful personnel. Be wary if they hurry
        you into buying something you don't want.
3.   A thorough guarantee and, even better, a repair shop on the
        premises.
4.   The best prices in town. Most good stereo dealers guarantee
        their prices. If you find a lower one, they'll refund the difference.

Keep your eye out for sales. Why not wait to buy your system at
the lowest price possible?

Also, remember that prices on stereo components are flexible. It's
one of the few businesses left where you can still bargain. If you find
a system you like, offer $50 less than the salesman is asking, or even
$100 less. Offer him cash on the spot. Offer to take it away right then
(stereo stores often have a space problem). Ask him to throw in a set
of earphones or a better cartridge. This kind of haggling is acceptable,
even necessary, if you're going to get the best deal possible.

Appearances

A good stereo should be heard and not seen. That's lucky, since most
stereo systems are a boon to the ear but a blight to the eye. There are
a few exceptions. The Bang & Olufsen, for example, is in the permanent design collection of the Museum of Modern Art. But beauty
is expensive and temperamental. The best-looking machines tend to
cost a fortune and break down often. Stick to basics. The idea is buy
a machine that reproduces sound, not a piece of furniture.

The problem of appearance is even more acute if your taste tends
toward the Bauhaus. Obviously, you should avoid those ungainly con-
soles in "Colonial," "Mediterranean," or "French Provincial." If you

look hard enough, you can find a few turntables and receivers that are designed simply, without a lot of wood trim. But what about the speakers? Unfortunately, the largest and most conspicuous component doesn't exist in Bauhaus designs. Unless you can afford to build your speakers into the wall or to construct your own cabinets, you're generally stuck with traditional-looking speakers. Just hide them as best you can.

A note of caution: speakers made from white plastic and mounted on trumpet pedestals are Buck Rogers, not Bauhaus.

Equally unacceptable are components that display all their working mechanisms. Turntables with see-through platters and speakers without grills are for display windows and industry trade shows. All that machinery calls unwanted attention to itself. The music is the message—not the mechanism.

In choosing a stereo, make the sound your first consideration. When you have a choice of cabinetry, pick real wood. American and Japanese manufacturers use walnut and mahogany. Europeans favor teak and rosewood. If all you can get is wood veneer or worse, fake wood, complain loudly. Write a letter. Sulk. But buy it anyway. The sound, after all, is most important.

Grills for speakers come in cloth or foam. Cloth is almost always better. Manufacturers have a bad habit of molding foam into bizarre shapes. Remember, as in all matters of style, simpler is better.

How Much Should You Spend?

Stereo systems come in all prices. You can spend as little or as much as you want. For good sound, the minimum is about $350. There is no maximum. How much should *you* spend?

Unless listening to music is your one great passion in life, be modest. Whatever adjectives the salesman may use, there really isn't *that* much difference between a moderately priced stereo and an expensive one. A higher-priced system will increase the *quantity* of the sound you hear, but it won't noticeably improve the *quality*. If you live in an apartment, you don't need an extra $500 in decibels. Save the money and satisfy your neighbors. A $500 system is all you *really* need.

Of course, an additional $1,000 will improve the sound of your records *somewhat*. If it doesn't, you're buying the wrong equipment. But unfortunately that additional expense will also do marvels for the pops, clicks, hisses, and other noise on your records. You'll hear *them* better than the music. Stick with a cheaper system, and you won't have to listen to more than you want to.

Recommended Systems

Here are some recommended systems in each of three price ranges: $300–400, $500–700, and $1,000 or over. Unfortunately, we can't tell you what *the* best instrument at any price range is. There's no such thing. Anyone who pretends to tell you is probably just telling you what brand he happens to sell or what brand he owns himself.

We've listed several brands of comparable quality within each price range. Choose a range, note the suggestion, then head for the nearest good stereo shop. Listen first to the speakers. Pick your favorite, then add the other components. Choose the turntable last. When you're finished you'll have a system that will sound good to anyone, but especially to you.

1. $300–400
        Turntable: BIC/BSR/Garrard
        Cartridge: Any major brand (beware of house brands)
        Receiver: 15 watt Marantz/Onkyo/Pioneer/Toshiba
        Speakers: Advent/Burho Acoustics/EPI/Infinity/KLH
2. $500–700
        Turntable: Dual/Philips/Technics
        Cartridge: Any major brand (beware of house brands)
        Receiver: 30 watt Marantz/Sansui
        Speakers: ADS/Ohm

3. $1,000 or Over
        Turntable: Denon/Micro-Seiki/Thorens
        Cartridge: Micro-Acoustics/Ortofon
        Receiver: 40–50 watt Luxman/Onkyo/Yamaha
        Speakers: Allison/Celestion/Cizek/JBL/Monitor Audio

The Ideal System

What if listening to music *is* your one great passion in life? What if you're willing to dress in rags, walk to work, live on bread and water, and sleep in a dingy tenement just so you can have the best sound money can buy? Well, here it is. Enough sound to impair your hearing permanently.

There are no choices here, just the best. The air is too rarified to support much variety. For the system we would buy if we had the money, the imaginary bill is $15,000. That's right, $15,000. But, of course, if you've come this far, money has lost all meaning.

Turntable: Denon 6700
Cartridge: Denon DL-103D or DL-103S
Head amplifier: Denon HA1000
Pre-amplifier: Luxman 5C50
Amplifier: 100 watts/channel Luxman 5M21
Tone control unit: Luxman 5F70
Tuner: Luxman 5T50
Speakers: Klipschorn
Center channel speaker: Belle Klipsch
Headphones: STAX SRX Mark 3
Digital time delay: ADS 10
Dynamic noise filter: Burwen 1201A
Tape deck: Revox B77
Cassette deck: Tandberg 340AM

Believe it or not, the ideal system could be even more expensive. If we'd looked for only the most expensive items—the showiest hardware, the largest speakers, the fanciest price tags—we could have assembled a system that cost at least twice as much. Even in this ideal system, we've listed the products that produce the *best* sound audible to the human ear, not the most expensive sound money can buy.

We also left out a few gadgets like the graphic equalizer and the peak indicator and substituted a few recently invented ones. The digital time delay machine, for example, uses a separate amplifier and set of speakers to recreate the echoes and other acoustical characteristics of a real performance. It can make your living room sound like a symphony hall, a recording studio, or a football stadium, depending on the record. We've also included a dynamic noise filter, a machine that removes the annoying hiss that plagues many systems of this quality.

Incidentally, we left out a "click and pop machine." This removes the pops and scratches of worn or imperfect records, all right, but—unlike the noise filter—it also removes some of the music. If you want to spend a lot of money on a stereo, try to spend it on items that will improve the *sound*. It's in questionable taste to spend more than you need to for a stereo. It's clearly in bad taste to spend as much as you can just for the show of it.

For More Information

The current issue of *Consumer Guide: The Best of Stereo/Hi-Fi Equipment* (New York: Publications International).

Building a Record Collection

Some activities are stylish because stylish people have always done them, like sailing. Some are stylish because they're creative, like writing and painting. Some are stylish because they're attractive, like dressing right and looking good.

Music is stylish on all three counts. It's been the passion of the privileged since ancient times, it's creative, *and* it's a delight to the ear. Music has been, is, and always will be an important part of the stylish life.

Any music will do. Pop, jazz, rock. Of course, some types of music are more stylish than others. Rock, for example, is more stylish than country western. Jazz more stylish than rock. But the most stylish music has always been classical. That's why we offer a guide to building a classical record collection. But remember, the idea is not to listen to classical music just because it's *stylish*. The idea is to learn to like classical music and then listen to it *because* you like it.

Of course, you may already like classical music. But what if you're a beginner? You've heard a few pieces of classical music on television, in the movies, or in friends' homes. Some you liked, some you found boring. To you, Rossini is the Lone Ranger, Mozart is Elvira Madigan, and Beethoven is anything that begins "ta ta ta *dum*."

Records are the answer. Start a collection of classical records. Keep it small at first. Buy just the things you know you like. Listen to them again and again. Learn to like the classical *sound*. Don't be discouraged if you don't go crazy over something the first time you hear it. Very few people do. Repeated listenings will reveal the greatness of any piece.

The Warhorses of the Classical Repertoire

The problem for the beginner, of course, is deciding where to begin. If you're a complete beginner, you don't know what you like. So how can you buy it? The answer is to start with the easy works—the ones that are rhythmically exciting or melodically memorable, the pieces they advertise on late-night television. These are the warhorses of the classical repertoire. It doesn't take any special training or culture to like them, just an ear and a heart.

Here is a selection of them. We list composer, title, record label, conductor and/or performers, and catalog number.

1. Johann Sebastian Bach: Brandenburg Concerti (ABC, Leonhardt, Leonhardt Consort, 2-ABC67020).
2. Ludwig van Beethoven: Symphony No. 5 (DGG, Kleiber, Vienna Philharmonic, DG 2530516).
3. Frederic Chopin: Polonaises (RCA, Rubinstein, 2-RCA LSC-7037).
4. Aaron Copland: Appalachian Spring (Columbia, Copland, Columbia Chamber Orchestra, Col. M-32736).
5. Antonin Dvorak: Symphony No. 9 (New World) (DGG, Giulini, Chicago Symphony, DG 2530881).
6. George Gershwin: American in Paris/Rhapsody in Blue Columbia, Bernstein, New York Philharmonic, Col. M-31804).
7. Wolfgang Amadeus Mozart: Concerti for Piano Nos. 17, 21 (DGG, Anda, Salzburg Mozarteum, DG 138783).
8. Wolfgang Amadeus Mozart: Magic Flute (DGG, Bohm, Berlin Philharmonic, 3-DF 2709017).
9. Wolfgang Amadeus Mozart: Symphonies Nos. 40, 41 (Jupiter) (DGG, Bohm, Vienna Philharmonic, DG 2530780).
10. Johann Pachelbel: Kanon (Angel, Marriner, The Academy of St. Martin-in-the Fields, Ang. S-37044).
11. Sergei Rachmaninoff: Concerto No. 2 in C for Piano/Preludes for Piano (DGG, Richter, Wislocki, Warsaw Philharmonic, DG 138076).
12. Maurice Ravel: Bolero, Rapsodie Espagnol/La Valse (DGG, Ozawa, Boston Symphony, DG 2530475).
13. Gioacchino Rossini: Overtures (including William Tell) (DGG, Abbado, London Symphony, DG 2530559).
14. Robert Schumann/Edvard Grieg: Concerti for Piano, (Philips, Bishop, Davis, BBC Symphony, DG Phi. 6500166).
15. Peter Ilyitch Tchaikovsky: Concerto No. 1 in B-Flat for Piano/Marche Slav (DGG, Richter, Karajan, Vienna Symphony, DG 138822).
16. Peter Ilyitch Tchaikovsky/Felix Mendelssohn: Concerti for

Violin (DGG, Milstein, Abbado, Vienna Philharmonic, DG 250359).
17. Peter Ilyitch Tchaikovsky/Ludwig van Beethoven: Overture 1812/Wellington's Victory (DGG, Karajan, Berlin Philharmonic, DG 2536298).
18. Antonio Vivaldi: Four Seasons (Nonesuch, Barchet, Tilegant, Southwest German Orchestra, None. 71070).

The Classical Top Twenty

The old warhorses are perfectly good pieces of music. Some are better than others, of course. Mozart's piano concerti are among the finest works of the period. Others are less awesome. Ravel's Bolero, for example, was never a great piece of music. Thanks to the Boston Pops Orchestra and its persistent renditions, however, the Bolero has become the goblin of classical music buffs. The first note is enough to make them scurry for cover.

But the only real problem with the old warhorses is that they're all the same. There are too many classical and romantic pieces, not enough medieval, Baroque, and modern ones. There are also too many instruments and not enough voices, too few choirs, songs, or operas. Note how few symphonies there are, how little chamber music or solo instrumental music. If you like classical music enough to listen to it seriously, you might as well learn the fullness of it throughout its history and in all its media.

The classical repertoire is enormous. It covers hundreds of years and would take almost that long to listen to. If you want to know classical music, try to get a sense of this rich tradition. Learn the fullness of its history (Renaissance, Baroque), the variety of its forms (opera, symphony, cantata), the diversity of its sound (solo voice, symphonic choir, string quartet). To help you do this, we've compiled a classical top twenty: twenty works chosen to represent different periods, different composers, different forms. The list is by no means complete, but it's a good beginning.

The Middle Ages and the Renaissance

1. Claudio Monteverdi: Madrigals (Philips, Leppard, Ambrosian Singers, 3-Phi. 6703035).
2. Giovanni Palestrina: Missa Papae Marcelli (DGG, Schrems, Regensburg Cathedral Choir, DG ARC-198182).

The Baroque Era

3. Johann Sebastian Bach: Brandenburg Concerti (ABC, Leonhardt, Leonhardt Consort, 2-ABC67020).
4. Johann Sebastian Bach: Toccata and Fugue in D for Organ (DGG, Walcha, DG ARC-198304).
5. George Frederic Handel: Messiah (Argo, Marriner, The Academy and Chorus of St. Martin-in-the-Fields. 3-Argo D18D-3).
6. Antonio Vivaldi: Four Seasons (Nonesuch, Barchet, Tilegant, Southwest German Orchestra, None. 71070).

The Classical Era
7. Ludwig van Beethoven: Sonatas for Piano Nos. 8, 14, 23 (Pathétique, Moonlight, Appassionata) (Philips, Arrau, Phi. 6599308).
8. Beethoven: Symphony (Choral), No. 9 (London, Solti, Chicago Symphony, 2-CSP-8).
9. Franz Joseph Haydn: Symphonies Nos. 103, 104 (Drum Roll, London) (DGG, Jochum, London Philharmonic, DG 2530525).
10. Wolfgang Amadeus Mozart: Concerti for Piano Nos. 17, 21 (DGG, Anda, Salzburg Mozarteum, DG 138783).
11. Wolfgang Amadeus Mozart: Don Giovanni (Angel, Klemperer, New Philharmonic Orchestra, 4-Ang S-3700).

The Romantic Era
12. Hector Berlioz: Symphonie Fantastique (DGG, Ozawa, Boston Symphony, DG 2530358).

13. Johannes Brahms: Quintet for Clarinet & Strings (DGG, Lester, Amadeus Quartet, DG 139354).
14. Frederic Chopin: Etudes (DGG, Pollini, DG 2530291).
15. Maurice Ravel/Claude Debussy: String Quartet (DGG, La-Salle Quartet, DG 2530235).
16. Franz Schubert: Quintet in A (Trout) (DGG, Gilels, Amadeus Quartet, DG 2530646).
17. Richard Wagner: Tristan and Isolde (DGG, Bohm, Bayreuth Festival, 5-DG 2713001).

The Twentieth Century
18. Béla Bartók: Concerto for Orchestra (London, Solti, London Symphony, Lon. 6784).
19. Gustav Mahler: Das Lied von der Erde (Philips, Baker, King, Haitink, Concertgebouw Orchestra, Phi. 6500831).
20. Igor Stravinsky: Rite of Spring (DGG, Karrajan, Berlin Philharmonic, DG 2530884).

Once you've digested these, you'll be ready for bigger things. All that listening will probably leave you with a good idea of what you like and what you don't like. Let that be your guide. Take what you like—a period, a composer, a form—and buy more of it. Don't worry if some famous names don't make your list of favorites. Besides, sooner or later your tastes will change and those names will reappear. Just remember, your likes and dislikes should determine the character of your library. Don't try to make it work the other way around.

Once you know where you're going, the best guide is the *Schwann Record & Tape Guide*. Published every month, it's a complete listing of all records still being issued. Look up your favorites and find a recording that suits you. The publishers of the Schwann catalogue also publish a list they call "A Basic Record Library." It's too long for the real beginner, but it can provide some helpful suggestions.

Choosing a Record

Unfortunately, the Schwann guide tells you both more than and less than you want to know. With exhausting comprehensiveness, it tells you everything that's available—fourteen complete recordings of the Brahms symphonies, dozens of 1812 Overtures, a score of Handel Messiahs, and pages of listings for the Brandenburg Concerti. If you don't already have a favorite conductor, symphony, or performer to look for, the profusion of available recordings is enough to discourage even the most enthusiastic beginner.

What are you looking for in a record? Three things: quality of performance, quality of recording, and quality of pressing. The Schwann catalogue doesn't rate records according to each of these tests, but it does often provide you with enough information to draw your own conclusions about a record's quality.

Quality of Performance.. The best way to ensure that you're buying a good performance is to buy only the best performers. After you've been listening to classical music for a while, you'll know who they are. You'll also begin to develop your own favorites. If you're still a beginner, try asking friends or the salesperson at the record store.

If you're still lost, follow this simple rule: The best performers generally record for the best recording companies. The best recording companies are Columbia, Angel, and RCA (in America); London, EMI, and Argo (in England); and Phillips, Deutsche Grammaphon, and Telefunken (on the Continent). We're not saying that you can't find great performances on other labels, or that all the performances on these labels are great. But you can be sure that these companies never record *bad* performances.

Quality of Recording. Even the greatest performance is wasted if it isn't recorded well. Unfortunately, there are many ways to record a piece of classical music badly. The orchestra drowns out the chorus, the chorus drowns out the soloist, the horns drown out the orchestra. If the recording was done in a large, empty hall, everything can be a muddle. If it was done in a soundproof studio, it can sound dry and dull—as if it were performed under a pillow. A great recording requires almost as much skill as a great performance, and it's considerably more expensive. Again, only the best recording companies have the expertise and the money to do the job right.

But not all the major companies do it equally well. American companies, primarily because of costs, don't take the care in recording that European companies do. There are a few exceptions. RCA, for example, has taken great care in its recordings of Horowitz and Rubenstein. Columbia recordings made prior to 1965 are also among the very best. But today, if you want to be *sure* of a good recording, the rule is to buy European.

Quality of Pressing. This is the least known aspect of buying records, yet it has the most to do with how the record sounds when you take it home and play it. Some records sound as clear as the actual performance, maybe clearer. No hum or hiss, just clean, bright sound. Others sound so bad that the quality of the performance or recording is irrelevant. All you can hear is clicks, hisses, and pops. The difference is in how the records are made, or "pressed." If the pressing is done carefully, using high grade vinyl under strict quality control, the record will be free of bumps, bubbles, and other irregularities that cause those annoying noises. If not, you might as well use them to line the litter box.

Unfortunately, this is another area where it's generally a bad idea to buy American. If there's any aspect of record making where American manufacturers are hopeless also-rans, it's the pressing. As a rule, they use lower-grade vinyl and spot-check their records carelessly. You can get a bad pressing on any label, but on American labels, the odds are better than even.

Phillips, a Dutch company, does the best pressings, followed closely by Deutsche Grammaphon, Telefunken, EMI, and Argo. Of course, you have to pay for the difference in quality. Foreign labels are significantly more expensive than domestic ones. But you get every cent's worth in better sound. If you *have* to worry about money, try the American budget labels, especially Odyssey and Nonesuch. The recording and pressing quality is on a par with the major American labels, but the price isn't.

What if the best performance isn't on the best label? What if the best performer—Horowitz, for example—records exclusively on a label with poor pressing quality—RCA, If you have to choose, do you go for the quality of the performance, the quality of the recording, or the quality of the pressing?

There's no easy answer. You just have to balance the alternatives for yourself. Of course, some performances are so good—Rubenstein playing Chopin on RCA, for example—that the recording and pressing are irrelevant. But if there is a *good* performance on a *good* label, you might prefer it to a *great* performance on an undesirable label. Fortunately, many of the best performances are also on the best labels.

For Further Assistance

To help the beginner find his way through the maze of possibilities, Penguin publishes a *Penguin Stereo Record Guide* (New York: Penguin Books, 1975) that takes up where the Schwann guide leaves off. It rates all the best recordings, giving them one, two, or three stars. Memorable recordings win an additional rosette. Because it's published in England, the Penguin guide includes many recordings not available in this country, but they are a small distraction. The object, of course, is to know the field so well you won't need a guide. But until then, the Penguin book is a good way to ensure that your collection is made up of only the best.

Chapter Ten:

Eating Out

Eating Out in Style

Of all your leisure time activities, eating out is probably the most frequent and the most important. Whether it's a quick bite before the movie or an elegant dinner after the concert, meals are often the focus of weekend socializing. If you're a businessman or professional who deals often with clients, meals are also an important part of the weekday routine. There's no counting the deals, agreements, and relationships—both social and professional—that have been consummated over good food and drink.

Because eating out is such an important part of the stylish life, you should take time to learn its ins and outs. In this chapter, we try to answer some of the basic and often mystifying questions: how to choose a restaurant, how to arrange an evening out, how to make sense of a menu, and how to order a wine. The key to eating out in style, like the key to doing anything in style, is to know what you're doing. Knowledge gives you confidence—and confidence is the essence of style.

Choosing a Restaurant

If you want to go out for dinner on the town, the first problem is finding the right restaurant. The easiest solution is to ask a friend. Just make sure the friend you ask knows something about food. After you've been eating out for a few years, you'll have your own list of favorites from which to choose.

What if your friends don't like restaurants? What if you just moved to town and you don't have any friends yet? Try your local tourist center or chamber of commerce. If you live in a big city, there's probably a monthly magazine that lists restaurants. But beware. Many of these publications sell their entries. A big restaurant can buy more than its share of space and superlatives. A small restaurant may not be able to afford a listing at all. This is particularly disturbing when you consider that most really good food is served at smaller establishments.

We can't give you a list. But we can provide you with a few guidelines for selecting a restaurant.

Check It Out Yourself

If you're taking friends or clients out to eat and you want to impress them, don't rely on luck. Check the restaurant out beforehand. Have lunch there by yourself first. Learn your way around. Get the *feel* of the place. Familiarize yourself with the menu, the specialties of the house, the location of the bathroom, the appropriate dress, the credit cards they take, and so on. This kind of familiarity will eventually make you and your guests more comfortable—an important part of any successful dinner.

If you're going out with close friends, you can afford to be more adventuresome. In fact, experimenting together is part of the fun. All you have to lose is the price of dinner. Friends won't be upset if the restaurant isn't as good as you'd hoped—and you won't be embarrassed. Another possibility is to consult your dinner companions before you choose a restaurant. Get their ideas. It's friendlier, of course. But you also won't find out too late that one of your guests is allergic to Chinese food. If you're going dutch, the decision *must* be mutual.

Size

If the choice is between a large restaurant and a small one, try the small one. If the choice is between a restaurant with an extensive menu or one with a limited menu, go for the limited menu. Why? Because that's the best way to ensure that your food will be freshly prepared from fresh materials. No matter how good a large restaurant is, if it offers a wide selection, most of the food is ready long before you order it. Before you even walk in the door, your vegetables are steaming, your soup is boiling, your fish is baking, and your sauce is warming. Of course, all restaurants do *some* advance preparation. They have to. But the less the better.

Even if the restaurant's menu is limited, size is still important. A large restaurant with a limited menu will have to prepare gallons of sauce and pounds of mousse. That kind of cooking is for the army, not for an elegant dinner. As much as possible, each meal should get the individual attention of the chef. And that's only possible if the restaurant is small and the food is prepared to order.

The worst combination is a large restaurant with an encyclopedic menu. As a rule, these are food factories, not restaurants, and your meal will look and taste like a production-line product—dressed-up McDonald's, not haute cuisine. Of course, these emporiums *do* have a legitimate purpose: There are a lot of people who need to eat. But don't be fooled. They're not serving fine food and you shouldn't be paying fine-food prices.

Here's a rule of thumb. A good chef should not (and usually cannot) prepare more than fifty dinners a night. Call the restaurant you're considering and ask them how many dinners they serve each evening and how many chefs work in the kitchen. If they're turning

out significantly more than fifty meals per chef, you know your meal
won't get the attention it deserves.

Be Flexible

A final word of advice: If you walk into a new restaurant and don't
feel comfortable there—if you don't like the looks of the place, or
if you don't think the service will be adequate—walk out. You should
never feel embarrassed about taking your business elsewhere. Just
remember your companions; consider whether they'll be embarrassed
before you take action.

Kinds of Restaurants

Eating out in style is like planning a vacation. The choice of restaurants is really a choice of countries. The variety depends on where
you live. In a large city, you can visit almost any corner of the globe.
In a small community, you may only have a choice of France, Italy,
China, and perhaps Mexico.

In some areas, regional history or local minorities may determine
the culinary alternatives: French food in Louisiana, Mexican in the
Southwest, Italian on the East Coast, Chinese on the West, and so on.
The proximity of the ocean can also make a difference: seafood
on the coasts, beef in the heartland. Know what's best in your area and
when it's best. When you travel, make it a point to familiarize
yourself with what's best in the area you're visiting. Knowledge,
especially inside knowledge, is always stylish.

Here is a brief introduction to the most important kinds of restaurants you'll have to choose from.

French. French cuisine is the most elaborate—and expensive—
in the world, so you'd better be prepared to pay accordingly. The
cuisines of other nations have their good points, but gourmets generally agree that French food is the best. And it's certainly the most
stylish. Like so many other aspects of the stylish life, French cuisine

is a classic; it's never wrong. Unless there's a good reason to be going someplace else, a French restaurant should always be your first choice, especially for entertaining clients or friends. That's why most of this chapter on eating out is devoted to the ins and outs of French cuisine.

Italian. Italian cuisine has long been undervalued in this country. Most Italian restaurants here serve basically *Sicilian* food: pizza, spaghetti, ravioli, or anything else made with pasta and tomatoes. Sicilian food is tasty, but it's only part of the story. Northern Italian food is much more varied and delicious, often without a trace of pasta or tomato. A good Italian chef can work wonders with seafood or veal that will dazzle even a Frenchman.

Chinese. Chinese cuisine probably offers the greatest variety of foods. The typical Chinese restaurant also maintains a higher minimum standard of quality than most other reasonably priced establishments. But it isn't just the food that draws people to Chinese restaurants; it's the friendliness. People often share dishes in a kind of culinary mix and match. Using chopsticks can be awkward but entertaining. The only disadvantage is that the standard of cleanliness in Chinese restaurants often leaves something to be desired. Avoid trips to the kitchen.

Japanese. Japanese food bears a superficial resemblance to Chinese, but as a rule it's not as consistently appetizing or varied. Appreciating dishes like Sashimi—that's *raw fish*—requires considerable training. For the less adventuresome, Japanese steak houses are recommended, not so much for their cooking as for the histrionic flair of the cooks. The only thing Japanese about them, however, is the Samurai technique of food preparation.

German. German food resembles other Eastern European and Russian cuisines in its extensive use of boiled meats, cabbage, and potatoes. But it usually has a finesse lacking in the others. If you're hungry, only an American steak house can fill you up as well as a German wursthaus. Try Wienerschnitzel, sauerbraten, and the many varieties of wurst, always accompanied by a fine German beer.

Middle Eastern. Middle Eastern food is easy to like. It won't offend even the most sensitive palate. Lamb, ground meats, rice, and yogurt are primary ingredients. None of these should cause you any trouble. Greek and Syrian restaurants tend to have similar menus, but the Syrians generally use more care and less olive oil. Begin your meal with Khomous—a spread made from chick peas and mashed sesame seeds—and unleavened Syrian bread.

Mexican. Although Mexican food has its enthusiasts, most experts don't even consider it a cuisine. However, the ranking of the experts will probably have little noticeable effect on your taste for tacos, tortillos, and refried beans, nor should it. But you might think twice before arranging a Mexican dinner with someone who may not share your enthusiasm.

American. There is no such thing as American cuisine. There are American *cuisines,* however, and they cover as broad a range as the American people. Many of our cuisines, like our people, are imported. But many of these have been around so long they might as well be indigenous. Every region has its own foods, its own specialties, its own cooking methods, and its own favorites: Maine lobster, California crab, Washington salmon, Southern fried chicken, Boston baked beans, corn-fed Kansas beef. They're all part of American cuisine, and only a fraction of it at that.

Of course, there's another American specialty that really *is* a national cuisine: highway food. Stop along any major American highway, close your eyes, take a bite, and you won't know where you are. If we have a national food, it's hamburger, and the national chef is Ronald McDonald. In fact, hamburger is quickly becoming the *inter*national food. Along with Coco-Cola, hamburgers have changed the eating habits of millions throughout the world. American highway food may not be the equal of French cuisine for subtlety and sophistication, but it certainly sells better.

Why mention McDonalds in a book on style? Simply to illustrate the point that style, in eating out or anything else, isn't simply a matter of money. If style is *simply* a matter of anything, it's a matter of being appropriate. And there are times when a quick, cheap meal is appropriate—not tasty, nutritious, or elegant—but appropriate.

Our list is hardly exhaustive. We haven't mentioned Spanish, Indian, Polynesian, Algerian, Scandinavian, South American, African, or Caribbean foods. The possibilities are limited only by your imagination, your location, and your palate.

How Much to Spend

There is a limit to what good food should cost. That limit is about $25 per person, depending on the wine. If you pay more than that, you aren't paying for the food. You're paying for atmosphere and prestige.

Of course, there are times when you *want* to pay for atmosphere and prestige. Perhaps you're closing a business deal or courting a prospective client. Perhaps it's your twenty-fifth anniversary. Or your daughter's wedding. Or *your* wedding. There are times when you don't just want to be fed; you want to be impressed. Or, more often, you want your guests to be impressed. On these special occasions, the sky's the limit.

Just keep two things in mind. First, make sure that you *do* get good food. All show and no substance is always in bad taste. Second, remember you're paying for the atmosphere and forget about getting your money's worth. No food is worth five dollars a bite.

Preliminaries

If you think a successful dinner at a good restaurant begins when the maître d' seats you, you're wrong. A *successful* dinner begins long before you enter the restaurant with the selection of the *right* restaurant for the occasion. But even after you've made a choice, the preparations are not complete. Here are some other decisions you should anticipate.

What Time to Eat

When you eat out, the timing is simple: the later the better. If the meal is the only event, be sure to give it the heart of the evening—nine to eleven. It's partly a matter of fashion and partly a matter of good sense. The fashion is European. For a variety of reasons, Europeans eat later than Americans. They take longer, later lunch breaks. That way, late dinners don't mean the alternate periods of starvation and indigestion for them that they often do for Americans. On the weekends, however, Americans become Europeans—at least in their eating schedules.

There's also some good sense behind the European rule. If you start at six, you'll be finished by nine, and then what are you going to do? It's too late for the theater. But it's too early for bed.

What if dinner isn't the evening's only activity? There's the theater, the symphony, or the movies. How can you eat fashionably late and still make it to an 8:00 curtain? You can't. But the solution isn't to swallow your style and arrive at an empty dining room at 5:30. Or, worse yet, grab something quick on the way to the theater. The solution is to eat even *later—after* the show. This will not only expand the evening in the right direction, it will give you something to talk about during the meal. Instead of trying to discuss what you've just seen and heard as you walk out of the theater in a crowd, you can linger over the details while you linger over your food and—ideally—over each other.

What to Wear

For better or worse, most good restaurants are less formal than they used to be. Saturday night is still black tie only at Maxim's. But almost any place else in the world, coat and tie will suffice. Nothing less, however; a good dinner deserves the appropriate dress. Calling ahead isn't enough. The restaurant will undoubtedly tell you what is *acceptable*—a far looser standard than what's appropriate or stylish.

If dinner is the whole evening, dress for the dinner. If it's dinner and something, dress for the something. It's impossible to overdress at a good restaurant. People will always assume you're coming from or going to a more important event.

Making Reservations

If you go to the trouble of choosing the right restaurant, don't show up without a reservation. On those rare occasions when you can't avoid it, a little financial friendliness to the maître d'—a couple of dollars will do—is an acceptable remedy. But don't be fooled by the movies. This is a last resort and it doesn't always work. Many maître d's are incorruptible autocrats. You may be sparking a scene more embarrassing than the one you sought to avoid. A little patience and a lot of deference will often do more than money.

But save yourself the awkwardness and the money by making a reservation. A day in advance is sufficient for most restaurants, but not all. Play it safe. Calling to make a reservation is also a good opportunity to deal with other matters. The wine you want may need to be decanted ahead of time. You may want a quiet table or one with a view. You may want a bottle of champagne chilled and waiting. Arrange the details in advance and the evening will unfold smoothly and elegantly.

Ordering the Meal

You've selected the right restaurant. You've made a reservation. And the time for the meal has arrived. We hate to say it, but your problems have just begun. Ordering a meal in style requires an expert knowledge of gourmet cuisine, of course, but also of psychology and even of high finance. You need to know how to order the meal, and also how to deal with the waiter, how to use the cutlery, how to pay the bill. In order to create a stylish meal, you must have every detail under control.

Dealing with the Waiter

In Europe, the model of good service is the invisible waiter. He brings the food, clears the table, and keeps the glasses filled without notice. His presence does not obscure vision or interrupt conversation. "Thank you's" are inappropriate because they acknowledge his activity.

Treat an American waiter this way and you're inviting Bordelaise onto your lap. There are, of course, some American restaurants where the service as well as the cuisine is in the European style. But most American waiters won't understand it if you ignore them. They appreciate "Thank you's" and compliments. Treat them accordingly.

European or American, a good waiter will anticipate your needs. You'll seldom have to get his attention. But when you do, use common sense. Don't call out, snap your fingers, or bang your glass. Tactics like these are for prison mess halls. Just catch the waiter's eye or lift your finger discreetly.

It's not just good manners to treat a waiter properly; it's good politics. Treat him properly and he'll serve you properly. You won't *have* to search for him every time you need your glass refilled.

Turn to the waiter for advice. You should never feel embarrassed about asking him for his recommendations. The waiter should know what the restaurant's specialties are. And if he doesn't happen to know what's fresh or what was just baked, he can certainly find out for you.

On the other hand, don't try to cultivate a lifelong relationship. He's busy, and you should be too. Save your conversation for your dinner companions. But a few words of appreciation—followed by a generous tip—will ensure that your next visit will be even more warmly welcomed.

Courses

If you're a meat and potatoes man, the question of courses can be new and confusing. Americans have simplified meals until there are really only two courses: the meal and the dessert. And even that division is more a matter of temptation than of taste.

When you eat out in style, things are not so simple. The classic French meal, for example, consists of seven courses, each served separately. Why such an elaborate scheme? For one thing, stylish meals are not just feedings; they're events. They're supposed to occupy an entire evening. For another, they allow you to sample a variety of foods. No single course is very big so you can't fill up on one or two items. A classic French meal is a far cry from an American steak dinner, when you're already filled with bread and salad by the time your steak arrives.

But even in a classic French meal, you have some flexibility. If you want the works, you can order a meal *prix fixe*, meaning that the number of courses and the price are set. But if you want to pick and choose, simply order *à la carte*. If you want *more* than seven courses, stretch the meal with sherbet. A small dish of sherbet (*sorbet*) between the fish and the entrée, or between the salad and the cheese, can aid digestion and clear your palate.

In any event, whether you eat them all or not, you should know the seven basic courses:

1. Soup
2. Appetizer
3. Fish
4. Entrée
5. Salad
6. Cheese
7. Dessert

Some Suggestions

Bread.   The meal begins with soup, not bread. Pay no attention to that basket of rolls, crackers, and other breadstuffs. The restaurant puts them there to tempt your taste buds and dull your appetite. They're afraid the entrée will be too small and you'll leave the table still hungry. The idea seems to be that a bloated customer is a happy customer. Besides, bread costs less than meat.

Choosing.   Order what you like. But try something new from time to time. Just don't order by the price list. The most expensive item isn't necessarily the best. Price depends on the demand, the preparation time, and the cost of the ingredients. Quality depends on the recipe, the talents of the chef, the care of preparation, and the freshness of the ingredients. They're not the same. If you prefer chicken to lobster, order chicken.

Variety.   The other consideration is variety. Mix it up. Order beef for an appetizer and fish for an entrée. Or vice versa. Remember that the purpose of having so many courses is to give you a variety of tastes and textures. If you're going to the trouble of having seven different courses, they might as well be different.

Salad.   American restaurants serve the salad first, partly to keep you occupied while the entrée cooks and partly to fill you up. Americans seem to like the idea. They've gone salad-crazy. Many seem to think that a long salad bar is the mark of a fine restaurant. If you plan to eat out in style, you'll have to fight this fetish for lettuce. A good French restaurant will serve the salad after the entrée and before the cheese course (or dessert) to clear the palate. The salad won't be elaborate, just a few leaves of lettuce or spinach. Why ruin a large meal by filling up on greens?

Dressing.   Even though you're in a French restaurant, don't order

"French" dressing. It's not French. The *real* French dressing, made from oil and vinegar, comes closest to what we call "Italian" dressing. Avoid anything else, such as Russian or Thousand Island. They're all too crude. That pungent taste that you love so much will turn your wine to water.

Coffee. If you want coffee, wait. The proper time for it is at the end of the meal (preferably with dessert). The only exception is breakfast. Why? Because the strong taste of the coffee deadens your taste buds. Considering the price you're probably paying, you might as well *taste* the food.

Culinary Terms

To enjoy eating out in style, you need to be relaxed and self-confident. Unfortunately, many people find it hard to relax in an elegant restaurant. The waiters are in black tie, the maître d' has an imperious foreign accent, and the prices on the menu look like misprints. It can be intimidating. In fact, in some cases it's *designed* to be intimidating.

One way to avoid being intimidated is to know what's going on. Of course, that can be difficult when everything seems to be going on in a foreign language. The menu, for example. If you don't read French, you may not be able to read the menu in a French restaurant. The difficulties are compounded by the fact that most French restaurants, with characteristic arrogance, refuse to provide translations of their menus. Even if you *do* read French—even if you know, for example, that *poulet* means chicken—you may not know the difference between the half-dozen chicken dishes listed. In that case, you're left to the mercy of the waiter. It's difficult to remain relaxed and self-confident when you feel like a child in the schoolroom again.

What we've provided below is a primer of French menus. We assume you already know, or can find out, the French names for all the basic foods: chicken, beef, veal, fish, and so on. We hope these additional terms will help you figure out how the foods are served.

Surprises have their place, but ordering an expensive meal shouldn't be a game of pin the tail on the donkey.

Garnishes. Garnishes are placed on or around a main dish for both flavor and decoration. Because dishes are often named after their garnishes, the names are a good indication of what you can expect inside. Here are a few of the more important ones:

1. *Bonne femme*: prepared with mushrooms.
2. *Duglère*: prepared with tomatoes and parsley.
3. *Florentine*: prepared on a bed of spinach, usually served with a cheese sauce.
4. *Niçoise*: prepared with olives, often with garlic and tomatoes.
5. *Perigord*: prepared with truffles, often with paté.

Sauces. Sauces are the *sine qua non* of French cuisine. But despite their great subtlety, they're remarkably easy to understand. Just remember that most sauces require what is called a "liaison," a base that binds the liquids together and enriches the flavor of the sauce. The most important liaison (other than the one you've planned *after* dinner) is a *roux*, made from butter and flour. There are three kinds of *roux*: white, blond, and brown, depending on what the cook adds to the two basic ingredients. Some frequently used sauces are:

1. *Béarnaise*: egg and butter with various spices.
2. *Béchamel*: white *roux* with milk.
3. *Brown Sauce*: brown *roux* with stock and vegetables.
4. *Chasseur*: brown *roux* with mushrooms and other vegetables.
5. *Demi-Glace*: brown *roux* with stock, vegetables, and Madeira.
6. *Espagnol*: tomato.
7. *Hollandaise*: egg and butter.
8. *Madeira*: Madeira wine.
9. *Mornay*: cheese.
10. *Velouté*: *roux* with stock instead of milk.

Cheeses

In any fine meal, cheese should be a separate course, served after the entrée or even after the salad, but before the dessert. Of course, the cheese course can also be combined with or even substituted for the dessert course. Try combining it with a fresh fruit, or with nuts, especially walnuts.

The place for cheese is on crackers—not bread, but unflavored and unsalted crackers. Remember, it's the cheese you want to taste. The two best crackers are Carr's Table Water Bisquits (obviously English) and Bremmer Wafers (if you prefer to buy American). If you insist on bread, a light French bread is best. Wonder Bread won't do.

Choose the accompanying wine with care also. If the cheese has a strong taste, choose a strong wine, a red Bordeaux, for example. Cheese and nuts at the end of the meal demand a good port.

Some cheese to look for:

1. Brie.
2. Blue (try Stilton or Pipot Creme).
3. Triple Crème (Boursault is the best).

Most good restaurants will carry these. Among the many cheeses to avoid are cheddar, Swiss, American, Gruyère, and Gouda. Mild cheeses are fine for grilled-cheese sandwiches, but they don't deserve the flattery of a good wine.

Cutlery

If the wine list, the waiter, or the menu doesn't intimidate you, the cutlery might. In many good restaurants, you'll find a dozen utensils spreading out from both sides of the plate, enough forks, spoons, and knives to set several places at home.

Where do you begin? Fortunately, the rule is simple. Start at the outside and work in. The first time you need a fork, take the one farthest to the left; the first time you need a spoon, take the one farthest to the right.

Easy enough—until you order soup and skip the appetizer. Then you're stuck with an unused fork. In a fine restaurant, you shouldn't have this problem. The waiter should clear away any unused cutlery before he serves the next course. But don't count on it. Few waiters are this knowledgeable or attentive.

If you're in a group, check yourself against someone you think is probably doing it right. If you're dining alone, or with people who are watching *you*, act with confidence. If you discover you have the wrong fork in your mouth, don't drop it on the floor. Don't lick it and put it back. Either put it down on your plate and begin again with the right one, or finish what you've started. An embarrassed scramble to do the right thing always attracts more attention than casually continuing to do the wrong thing.

The Final Reckoning

Paying the bill is the last and often the least enjoyable part of dining out. Don't let it be. A little careful advance planning is all it takes to end the evening in style.

Let everyone know in advance that you're paying the bill. Fights over the check may seem friendly and fun, but more often they're awkward and embarrassing. Make your intentions to pay clear when you extend the invitations. If your invitation didn't make your intention clear, your behavior should. Almost invariably, the person who pays the check is the person who invites the guests, makes the reservations, orders and tastes the wine, and deals with the waiter. As a safety measure, let the waiter know from the start that you're the host.

The solution is more complicated if it was a group decision to eat out. But don't make it more complicated than it has to be. Don't squabble over shares. You're supposed to be enjoying a dinner out, not conducting an audit. Divide the bill by the number of people, then designate someone to collect the shares and pay the waiter. This means, of course, that some will pay for more than they ate, some for less. The person who ate chicken will end up paying for part of the next person's lobster, but the difference is not worth a full-scale reenactment of the meal. Besides, the balance will probably fall the other way the next time.

Keep money out of sight. The less time and attention devoted to paying the bill, the better. This rule is easy to observe if you have an account at the restaurant or if it accepts credit cards. Otherwise, try to establish your credit in advance so you can pay by check. If all else fails, bring cash, lots of cash, twice as much as you think you'll need. Nothing will destroy the elegance of the evening or your poise faster than having to borrow money from your guests.

Don't be stingy. The 15 percent tip is a *rule*, not an option. Of course, like any rule, it has some exceptions. If the service was particularly good, 20 percent is in order. If the service was dismal, 10 percent, but only if the service was *dismal*. Slow service, occasional inattention, cold entrées, and other minor irritations do not constitute dismal service. Bordelaise in the lap, intentional slights, and frequent snarls do. But even for these outrages, 10 percent is the minimum. If it's a matter of pride, go ahead and leave less. Leave *nothing*. But don't plan on coming back any time soon.

For More Information

Craig Claiborne, *Craig Claiborne's Favorites from The New York Times*, four volumes (New York: Times Books, 1975, 1976, 1977, 1978).

Craig Claiborne, *The New York Times Cook Book* (New York: Harper & Row, 1961).

Prosper Montagné, *Larouse Gastronomique* (New York: Crown Publishers, 1961).

Irma S. Rombauer and Marion Rombauer Becker, *Joy of Cooking* (Indianapolis, Indiana: Bobbs-Merrill, 1931).

Selecting the Wine

So you've ordered the meal. Now you're perusing the wine list, trying to make some sense out of it. In a big, fancy restaurant, where the list is the size of a telephone book, this can be difficult. It can also be intimidating.

Of course, a waiter or wine steward is often helpful, but you shouldn't *have* to rely on his advice. If the wine steward is sick or your waiter is ignorant, you can't wait for divine intervention. With your attractive dinner partner watching and the waiter's pen poised, you don't want to be frantically trying to remember whether it's red wine or white that's served with veal. The purpose of this section is not to make you an expert. It's to keep you from feeling like a fool.

Red, White, or Rosé?

If nothing else, you should know what *color* wine to order. Chances are you already know the basic rule: red wine with red meat and white with fish or fowl. Some people consider rosé (pink) a compromise between red and white that can go with anything. Actually, rosé is a third kind of wine, not a cross between the other two. It goes well with nothing. It's a compromise only in the sense that it's not as good as either white or red.

The basic rule may seem simple. But no rule can stay simple for long, and winemaking is a very old enterprise. In fact, the rules about what to drink with what have developed over the years to the point that there's an appropriate wine for almost every dish. Heaven forbid that you should drink the same wine with beef Stroganoff that you drink with beef sukiyaki. Everyone knows that a red Burgundy does wonders for *coq au vin* but absolutely destroys chicken curry, and so on. If you aspire to be a wine expert (an oeneophile), these pieces of the Grail may interest you. Otherwise, you may safely ignore them.

Most of us mortals can survive knowing only the basics. But it also helps to know the rationale behind the basics. It's really very simple. The wine you drink should complement the food you eat. Just as foods have different tastes, wines have different tastes. The object is to get the right combination. If the wine is too strong, you won't be able to appreciate the taste of the food. But if the food is too strong, you won't be able to appreciate the taste of the wine. That's why red wines, usually strong, are drunk with *strong* foods. Delicate white wines are best for *subtle* foods.

Does it matter whether you follow the rules or not? Are you committing some unpardonable *faux pas* if you drink red wine with your oysters or white with your steak tartare? Well, yes and no. What you drink is, in the end, a matter of personal preference. As long as you know you're breaking the rules, go ahead and order whatever you like with whatever you like. If the waiter or the man at the next table gives you a snooty grimace, ignore him.

On the other hand, whether you're eating in a fine restaurant or at a friend's house, someone is going to a lot of trouble to cook your meal. Great cuisine is an art. Even if you don't enjoy it, you should appreciate it. Ordering a red wine with a carefully prepared, subtly flavored fish is like pouring ketchup on it. Your chances of tasting the fish are about the same. Many French chefs would kill for less.

As in all matters of style, there's a reason for the classic approach. The better you understand *why* the experts prefer different wines for different foods, the more you'll agree with them. Polyester may feel fine to a man who's never worn anything else. But let him walk around for a while in a good wool suit and he'll never go back. The same is true of wines. The more you know about them, the more you'll want only the right one.

What if you and your dinner partner order something different? What if you want steak and she wants oysters? One solution is to order two wines: a small bottle of white for her, a small bottle of red for you. All too often in this situation, people compromise on a rosé, as if rosé were half white and half red. It isn't. If you want to compromise, try a light red wine, a good Beaujolais, for example. It won't do wonders for either meal but it won't destroy one of them. It's also friendlier than ordering two bottles. Companionship, after all, is as important as taste.

Place of Origin

The best way to get to know wines is by their "address," their place of origin. Where were the grapes grown and processed? A wine's address consists of the country, the region, and the field where it was made. All three should appear on the wine list and on the label.

Tradition has it—and many people, especially French people, agree—that French wines are the best. We take exception. Some of the best wines today are American—Californian, that is. In fact, there is actually a *larger* stock of medium-priced American wines. In case you harbor any doubts, you should be aware that the products of California vineyards have tricked some of the most renowned French wine connoisseurs in blind testing.

There's a good reason why experts have a hard time telling the difference between American and French wines. The two have common roots, so to speak. When Americans began growing wine grapes in the nineteenth century, they went to France for the original plantings. Then, in the 1870s, Europe was hit by a devastating blight that killed almost every grapevine in France. French grape growers had to come to *California* in search of roots to graft their grape varieties onto. Frenchmen will argue to the death, of course, that climate, soil conditions, harvesting techniques, and the beauty of the French language are what really make French wines superior. Needless to say, such claims of French superiority are widely (and characteristically) exaggerated.

To help you distinguish one wine from another, the French have a system of government wine control. Every wine that passes a minimal inspection is given the label "*Appellation Controlée.*" The idea is to restrict wine labeling so that it accurately reflects the area of origin. The more specific the area of ground indicated on the label, the better the wine is supposed to be. This isn't always the case, but the French play the averages. Implied in any *Appellation Controlée* label are laws concerning grape varieties, maximum allowable yields, methods of pruning, and ageing.

The only other label is the highly sought after "*Grand Cru*," awarded only to a handful of the best Burgundy and Bordeaux wines.

In typical, orderly German fashion, the government in Germany ranks all German wines by minute gradations in quality. The Germans have no less than five different classifications of "*Qualitäts Wein*" (quality wine). Beginning with the most modest and culminating with the finest, they are:

1. Kabinett
2. Spätlese
3. Auslese
4. Beerenauslese
5. Trockenbeerenauslese.

Categories 3 and 4 occasionally have the word "eiswein" attached. This means that the grapes were partially frozen when picked, which gives them an interesting intensity of taste. Categories 4 and 5 are very scarce and very expensive.

Germany is best known for its light, slightly sweet sipping and light-food wines. Liebfraumilch is the most famous (or infamous) example.

Wines are known not only by their country but by their *region* within the country. You've certainly heard a wine referred to as a Burgundy or a Bordeaux. These aren't brand names; they're famous winemaking regions in France. In fact, learning wines is basically a matter of learning geography.

Bordeaux and Burgundy are the regions that generally produce the finest French wines. The valleys of the Rhône and Loire rivers are also famous wine-producing areas. All four regions produce both red and white wines. If you know those eight varieties, you know the most important French wines.

Italian wines are also known by region. Four whites and five reds head the list:

Italian White Wines	*Italian Red Wines*
Chianti	Chianti
Soave	Barolo
Orvieto	Gattinara
Frascati	Valpolicela
	Barbera

As you can see, Chianti produces good red as well as white.

The story is different in America. The best American wines are called *varietals*, meaning they're named after the variety of grape used in making them, not after the region where they grow. Still, tradition has it that the best California wines grow in the Napa and Sonoma valleys, or, more generally, in the vineyards northeast of San Francisco.

Wait. There's more. Even if you know the difference between the wines of different countries or even different regions within a country, there's still more to learn. A *real* wine expert can distinguish different *fields* within a region: which fields grow the best grapes, which fields bottle the best white, and so on. This is further than any reasonable man need go. But if you wish to, there's a book you can buy: *Hugh Johnson's Pocket Encyclopedia of Wine* (New York: Simon and Schuster, 1977). After you've read it, start sampling wines yourself. As studies go, sampling wines ranks pretty high.

Vintage

Two bottles of wine can come from the same country, the same region, even the same field, and still be completely different wines. The difference is age. That's why every bottle is marked with its year and why every great wine connoisseur knows the great dates—vintages— better than his children's birthdays.

Why does age make such a difference? It's largely a matter of rain. There's more of it during some years than during others. But the important factor isn't just the overall amount of rain; it's the *number* of days it rains—the number of *gris* or "gray" days. It's also *when* the rain takes place. Other climatic conditions—wind, temperature—count as well.

As in all wine matters, you could spend the rest of your life memorizing the details. But all you really need to know is that 1966, 1970, 1975, and 1976 were great years for Bordeaux; that 1967, 1971, and 1973 were pretty good; that 1969 and 1974 were problem years; and that 1968 and 1972 were disasters. If you hate memorizing dates, you can find the best vintages for all French and Italian wines printed in handy wallet-sized cards at most good wine stores. If you want to know more, refer to Johnson.

A word of caution. If the waiter brings you a bottle of 1977 Beaujolais, don't make a scene insisting on something older. Some wines, like Beaujolais, are supposed to be "young." Two years old is about the maximum.

How Much to Spend

How much you spend on your wine depends on how much you spend on your meal. Let the two complement each other in price as well as in taste. Admittedly, a $50 bottle of Chateau Lafite Rothschild will do a lot for a Big Mac at a nearby McDonalds, but it will do a lot more for sole amandine at the Four Seasons. If you order a six-course meal at a fashionable restaurant, don't comb the wine list for the lowest price. It's inappropriate and, if you're on an expense account, unnecessary.

What is an appropriate price? The following list will give you some idea:

If the meal costs:	The wine should be:
$5–10	½ carafe of house wine, $2.50–4.50
$10–15	Good Italian wine, $6–8
$15–25	Good French wine, *Appellation Controlée,* $6–13
$25–50	*Grand Cru,* from a good year, $13 and up
$50 and up	*Grand Cru,* from a great year, $20 and up

The Ritual of Tasting

Selecting a wine is not the last of it. After you've selected it, you must taste it. Most people are familiar with the ritual: Even the waiters at the Holiday Inn have been trained to open the bottle and pour a sip or two into the host's glass. Actually, few people *really* know what to do at this point. But most can fake it well enough. They look at the wine carefully, taste it, wait a few seconds, then nod their heads. What they're usually thinking during those few seconds—along with the waiter and their guests—is, "What do I say if I don't like it?"

The answer is, not much. The ritual of tasting is generally just that —a ritual. There are several things you can do to lend a little substance to the whole procedure, however. When the waiter or the wine steward shows you the bottle before opening it, look at it. Check to make sure it's the wine you ordered: the same vineyard, the same year. When he hands you the cork, check to make sure it's not dry or crumbly, a sign that air has entered the bottle and probably spoiled the wine. Smelling the wet end is another way to tell whether the wine has turned to vinegar because of a leak.

Once the waiter has poured a small amount into your glass, smell again for souring. Of course, if you're a connoisseur, you'll also be able to tell something about the quality of the wine from its *bouquet* (French for smell). Don't be ashamed if you can't. And don't pretend that you can.

If the wine is white, hold the glass by the stem. White wine is served chilled, and you don't want to lower the temperature by cupping the bowl of the glass in your warm palm. If the wine is red, turn it slowly in the glass. This supposedly releases the bouquet. A warning, however. People who really know what they're doing can turn wine with the slightest movement of the wrist. If you're a beginner, you may have a hard time getting it going. You won't fool anybody about your expertise by turning the wine awkwardly. Better to leave it be.

Your first sip should be small. Remember, you're tasting the wine, not quenching a thirst. Wash the wine around in your mouth for a few seconds. *Taste* it. If you like it, take a second sip.

The only legitimate reason to return a wine is that it has soured. And you should be able to tell that long before you get to the sipping stage. A restaurant will not hesitate to accept a returned bottle if the wine is bad. Of course, most fine restaurants will not refuse to accept a returned bottle no matter what your reasons for returning it. But you should never take advantage of their graciousness merely to impress your dinner guests with the sensitivity of your palate. After all, you *ordered* the wine and you should have known what you were getting.

Some helpful hints:

Beware the wine steward. Most great restaurants do not have wine stewards (*sommeliers* in French). Both the maître d' and the head waiter know about the restaurant's own wine cellar and probably a lot about wines in general. Many mediocre restaurants that *aspire* to greatness install a wine steward and hang a cup around his neck (until modern hygiene laws intervened, the cup was used to taste the wine). But in most cases he's either a busboy or their most distinguished-looking waiter dressed up for the role. Of course, there are a few wine stewards who actually know their business. Consider yourself fortunate indeed to find one.

If the waiter or the wine steward opens the bottle of red wine and places it on the table without offering a taste or pouring it, don't do it yourself. He has left the wine there to "breathe." You may have laughed the first time you heard that wine breathes, but it's no joke. Many people who complain about the bitterness of a red wine when they taste it are complimenting it by the time the meal is over. They think it's because any alcohol tastes better the more you drink it. Actually, it's because the wine has been allowed to breathe. It's probably best just about the time they're finished with it.

A final word. It is acceptable to dispense with the ritual entirely. If you're deep in conversation, don't feel compelled to take time off for the ritual. Just tell the waiter to fill the glasses. If the wine turns out to be bad, you can still send it back. You don't forfeit your right to reject the bottle by waiving your right to taste it. This may be of some comfort if you're one of the many people who find the whole procedure awkward and pretentious.

Aperitifs and Champagnes

Whites, reds, and rosés are called table wines, because you drink them at your table with your meal. Table wines are the most important, most common, and most complicated wines, but they're not the only ones. There are also aperitifs and champagnes.

Aperitifs are drunk *before* dinner, in lieu of mixed drinks. In England, *the* traditional aperitif is sherry. The continent offers a much wider assortment. From Italy, there are vermouths flavored with seeds and nuts: Campari and Cinzano, for example. From France, there are sweet vermouths (Dubonnet) and citrus-based vermouths (red and white Lillet).

There are also the *anise*-flavored drinks, Pernod and Anisette. These are basically legal versions of absinthe, a very popular drink that was banned when officials discovered it did terrible things to the nerves. Absinthe is what all the dazed figures are drinking in the paintings of Toulouse-Lautrec, Degas, and Manet.

Champagne, like cheesecake, comes two ways: sweet and heavy (*brut*) or dry and light (*sec*). The choice is yours. Champagne also comes pink, but that's no choice. Mae West drinks *only* pink champagne. Need we say more?

A true champagne comes only from Champagne, the French region where the wine was developed. Californian, Italian, and Spanish versions won't do. In fact, the winemakers of Champagne are mad at American growers for even using the name. They were once so mad that they sued (and lost). They think the American product should be called sparkling wine, or perhaps just plain "bubbly."

The two best *real* champagnes are probably Dom Perignon and Piper-Heidsieck. Paul Roger is almost as good and much cheaper, not because it's inferior champagne, or even because the company spends less on advertising. It's cheaper because Ian Fleming decided to have James Bond drink Dom Perignon instead.

In America, champagne is a celebration drink, uncorked for weddings, birthdays, anniversaries, graduations, even divorces—any special occasion. For one thing, champagne is a quick, efficient, and lethal yet legal high. It's also relatively expensive as wine goes. But champagne was originally just another dessert wine, often served with cheese and fruit at the end of a meal. Special occasions called for a vintage *red* wine.

But don't worry about the historical distinctions. In this country, champagne is *always* correct, before, during, or after dinner, for every day use or for that grand occasion. If you can afford it, champagne is always in style.

For More Information

Hugh Johnson, *The World Atlas of Wine*, rev. ed. (New York: Simon and Schuster, 1978).

Hugh Johnson, *Wine*, rev. ed. (New York: Simon and Schuster, 1975).

Pamela Van Dyck Price, *The Taste of Wine* (New York: Random House, 1975).

Terry Robards, *The New York Times Book of Wine* (New York: Avon, 1976).

CHAPTER ELEVEN:

Travel

Traveling in Style

During the late nineteenth century, young men of means filled the time between school and career with The Grand Tour, a leisurely trip through the Continent that took anywhere from three months to an entire year. The Grand Tour was considered an important part of a person's education, an essential element in the making of a stylish man.

Times have changed, of course. Now, if you have a good job, chances are you can afford to travel. In fact, in some jobs you *have* to travel. The successful man often makes ten, twenty, or even thirty business trips a year before he ever gets around to "vacationing."

We're not talking about old-fashioned traveling salesmen, either. In most professions, travel—whether it's to a one-day meeting or an all-week convention—has become a part of the job.

But even once-a-week business trips are no substitute for traveling at vacation time. Of course, today's vacation is a far cry from The Grand Tour. Not even the very rich can afford to travel for three months at a time, and taking off for an entire year is called retirement, not travel. The typical vacation is now two weeks—the most time a man can take off from work without returning to discover that he's been replaced.

The point is to know how to get the most out of your travel with the least trouble. After all, if you only have two weeks to relax away from the office, you don't want to spend half the time waiting for that crucial thing—a passport, say—that you left behind. The same is true for business trips. If you know the right steps—the right way to get there, the right place to stay, the right things to take—going to a conference in another city will be a pleasure, maybe even an adventure, and not just business as usual.

What to Do

What you do on a trip—whether it's for business or pleasure—will determine whether that trip is a success. We're not talking about the general purpose of the trip: "seeing" Paris, closing a business deal in Chicago, or opening your mind to Italian opera. We're talking about the way you go about accomplishing your general purpose: using the right means of transportation, setting the right pace, seeing the right things in just the right way. Knowing what to do on a trip, and how to do it, is the difference between just traveling and traveling in style.

Don't Take Tours

When you go abroad, whether it's for a two-day business meeting or a two-week frolic, avoid tours. You've seen them advertised, no doubt. Prepackaged trips with air transportation, cocktail parties, guided tours, even local atmosphere assembled for you like a frozen dinner at the supermarket. The only time to take a tour, like the only time to buy a frozen dinner, is when you can't make one for yourself.

Half the fun of seeing the sights in a foreign place is buying the guidebooks, learning about the monuments, reading the maps, figuring out the bus system, asking directions, and then finally experiencing them. All this may sound too much like work. If it's a business trip, you may already have all the work you want. If it's a vacation, you're probably trying to avoid work altogether. But if you do it right, a vacation is one place where work *is* relaxation. It's part of the experience, part of the enjoyment, and part of the memory. Paying a tour company to arrange a trip for you is like paying someone to eat a meal for you. You're missing the point.

What you really want is an *experience,* something you'll remember and enjoy long after you've lost the pictures. Seeing the sights is an important part of that experience, but there's a lot more. Leave your efficiency in your briefcase, even if it's just for an afternoon, and really *see* the place for yourself. Sign up for a tour and you'll only see the sights.

See the Country

There are many ways to get around a foreign country besides a tour bus. By far the worst is to fly from city to city. Of course, if you're on a business trip and need to make several stops in a short time, you may have no choice. But how much of a country can you see from 30,000 feet? Unless you're fortunate enough to pass the Alps, you might as well be flying over Kansas, Iowa, or Lake Erie.

A second and far better way to get around is by train. Most Americans are unfamiliar with the delights of train travel—even those who ride a train every morning. In America, railroads were eclipsed long ago by cars, buses, and planes. But in Europe, train travel is still in its golden age. Trains are clean, well-designed, convenient, inexpensive, and almost always on time.

Almost every country in Europe has rail passes for short or long periods and you can't beat the prices. Why watch clouds when you can watch a whole continent pass by? You'll find that the trains are also surprisingly comfortable and clean in many less developed countries, although first class passage is essential. Also, be prepared for crowds in the station.

But the very best way to see a country is by car. Take a plane and you see airports. Take a train and you see train stations. But take a car and you see the people: where they live, where they work, how they play. You become part of the country's daily life, not just another traveler in areas set aside for travelers. This is as true for the businessman with an off-day or a free weekend as it is for the vacationer.

Car rentals are expensive all right, but so are plane and train travel when you add up the costs of getting around inside the city. If you're paying for it yourself, go for the cheapest rates: Auto Europe when in Europe, and the budget companies when in the United States. Neither Hertz nor Avis is number one, and neither really tries harder when it comes to price. If you're planning to buy a foreign car, wait and plan a trip around it. Depending on the model you buy, you'll save enough on the price of the car to pay most of your expenses, and, of course, you won't have to pay transportation costs while you're there.

Pace Yourself

A stylish trip is always well-paced. Not too short, not too long. Not too sleepy, not too hectic. Of course, if you're taking a business trip, you may not have control over the pace. If you have to be back at the office in two days and you have to see ten people, pacing isn't your problem—planning is.

If you're taking a nonbusiness trip, the "right" length—conveniently—is two weeks. Any shorter than that, and you'll be back on the job before you really unwind. Too much longer, and you may begin to get bored with hotel rooms, restaurant food, historic buildings, sandy beaches, or your traveling companions.

Of course, the right length for a trip, business or pleasure, depends to some extent on the individual. Some hardy souls can persevere for months at a time. We wouldn't want to discourage some new Lawrence of Arabia from making an entire life of travel. But you know you've had enough when you're sitting in an office overlooking the Roman Forum and all you can think about is the next meal.

How much you do is as important as how long you stay, especially if it's your first visit. Don't be terrified by the thought of missing something. So many first time travelers are. Don't get up at the crack of dawn, crowd the day with appointments or sightseeing or both, then grab five hours of sleep before doing the same thing all over again. Chances are, you won't be able to keep this up for more than a day or two.

If your schedule permits, it's much better to spread the same activities out over several more leisurely days. Cut your normal activity by at least half when you're abroad. Never plan more than half a day of important meetings, active sightseeing, shopping, or traveling. Save time for rest, for an afternoon nap, or for an occasional quiet evening reading in the hotel. You may not like the idea of reading in your hotel room while all that exotic nightlife is happening around you. But remember, a trip is not a game of beat-the-clock. Without rest and a chance to reflect, you may end up doing more and accomplishing less.

Be Flexible

Don't be flustered if an unexpected turn of events upsets your carefully laid plans. Make the most of it. Remember, flexibility is not just a matter of planning; it's a state of mind. It's being ready to cancel the next stop on your schedule because you haven't made the most of this one. If you're vacationing, it's lingering in a place you love and not thinking about the places you're missing.

Where to Stay

When you travel in style, whether it's to Europe for the summer or Baltimore for the afternoon, *where* you stay is as important as what you do. In fact, where you stay may help determine what you do.

This is especially true abroad. One of the best ways to find good shops, restaurants, and activities in a new city is to ask the staff at your hotel. Ask the bell captain in a modern luxury hotel, and he'll give you modern luxury answers—the stores, restaurants, and activities he recommends to thousands of other American tourists. Ask the proprietor of a small European hotel or *pension,* on the other hand, and he'll probably tell you where *he* goes when he wants to buy a present, order a meal, or have a good time. Two people who visit Germany at the same time but who stay in two different hotels will see two very different Germanies. If you know how you want to see a country, make sure your accommodations are a help, not a hindrance.

Of course, there are reasons why you should pick your hotel accommodations carefully that have little to do with style. If you spend a long day at business meetings in London or sightseeing in the jungles of Zaire, it's good to know that a comfortable room awaits you. The more exotic and rigorous your itinerary, the more important this becomes.

In choosing a place to stay, as in almost everything else, style isn't simply a matter of money. Of course, you (or your company) *can* spend a fortune on the finest, most stylish accommodations—the Pierre in New York, for example. But fortunately, you can spend more modest amounts yet still find stylish accommodations. The *character* of the place, not the cost, is the key.

Here are the major kinds of accommodations you should consider, beginning with the most expensive and descending, with relief, to the most reasonable.

Country Retreats and Castles

Some European hotels are so good they're worth a trip across the Atlantic. They are usually small, independently owned hotels in western Europe converted from old castles, monasteries, and manor houses. They're not just places to stay; they're reasons for going.

Imagine a turreted castle overlooking the sea, a white and gold palace surrounded by formal gardens, a country house set amid green pastures and woods, ancient ruins, peacocks on the lawn, swans in the pond, breakfast on the terrace, tea in the garden, and dinner to a string quartet. It may sound like a fantasy or a Hollywood extravaganza, but it's not. These are real places—places where you can go and experience aristocratic Europe as it was when America was still a colony and the peasants were not yet grumbling.

So if you've ever dreamed of retiring to a castle in Scotland, a French chateau, or a royal hideaway, the chance is now yours. Try the beautiful Inverlochy Castle nestled at the foot of Ben Nevis, the highest mountain in the British Isles. Or stay at the exquisite Palace Hotel do Buçaco in the forests of Portugal, where the wine is made on the castle grounds and guests sleep in the king's suite. You don't even have to start a revolution. Just make a reservation. If either hotel is booked full, try one of the 280 hotels and guest houses that belong to the Relais et Chateaux, the largest association of these rare and delightful retreats. For more information, write Relais et Chateaux, 17 Place Vendôme F, 75001 Paris, France.

Oh yes, the price. Every silver lining has its dark cloud, and every fantasy has its price. This one will cost you between $100 and $150 per person per night, depending on the place and the time of year. This may seem high, but remember, the price includes a palatial room and two exquisite meals, breakfast and dinner. Stay in a good hotel, eat two good meals, and you'll only save, at most, forty or fifty dollars. As fantasies go, this one is a bargain.

Our second choice for stylish, out-of-the-way accommodations is Spain. Spain is still the mecca for travelers who want to live like princes on a young professional's budget. The Spanish government runs a system of hotels called *paradors* converted from historic buildings. They're not quite as grand as the Buçaco Palace or the Relais hotels: The rooms are more modern, the meals less elegant, and they don't have the same personal touch. But there's still food for fantasy: crumbling battlements, baronial halls, spacious banquet rooms, and historic vistas. Better yet, the price is realistic: about $30 per person per night for lodging and food. Write the Spanish National Tourist Board or Iberia Airlines in New York.

The Grand Hotels

But what if you love the city? What if all your appointments are downtown? After all, *paradors*, castles, and retreats may be in the country, but most businesses are not. Or maybe all that pastoral serenity would bore you to distraction. Maybe you prefer museums, interesting shops, and a wicked nightlife to clean air, lush scenery, and aristocratic ease. But you still want Old World charm and luxury. Take heart. You can have *both*—if you're willing to pay.

The answer is a grand hotel—a hotel with rooms so beautiful, food so exquisite, and service so elegant, it's really more like a busy palace than a common hotel. Like country retreats, grand hotels are the stuff of fantasies. They're also disappearing quickly. Here are some of the fabulous remaining few:

Paris: The Bristol or The Ritz
London: The Berkeley or Claridge's
Rome: Hassler Villa Medici
Vienna: The Imperial
Berlin: Bristol Kempinski
Munich: Vier Jahreszeiten Kempinski
Madrid: The Ritz
New York: The Pierre or The Sherry Netherland

Of course, if you're spending three weeks in Europe, you might think twice about a grand hotel—unless somebody else is footing the bill. At $100 a night, you can run up a grand bill even if you never order room service. For a long stay, find more reasonable, if less sumptuous, accommodations elsewhere. But for the occasion of a lifetime, an important deal, or a special event, indulge in a day or two of real splendor. These heights of style and luxury, like the grand hotels themselves, will soon vanish.

Modern Hotels

In Europe and the rest of the world, beware of "modern" hotels. "Modern" and "luxury modern" are really just code words for "American." Hotels that bear these labels will make you feel so much at home you might as well never have left. In fact, many of them *are* American. You can walk into the bathroom and find towels marked Hilton or Holiday Inn. Why suffer jet lag for that?

If you're going to Europe, there's no reason to stay in an American hotel. If you want to stay in an American hotel, stay in America. They're cheaper and more convenient over here. Remember, where you stay should be as much a part of your visit as what you see.

Of course, modern American hotels do have their place—even in Europe. If you arrive in a strange city early in the morning, exhausted from an all-night flight, you may prefer to shower, sleep, and save the local flavor for the next day. If so, make a reservation at a good modern hotel for the first night, then get up the next morning and search for more authentic accommodations.

If you're on a business trip, local flavor may be the last thing on your mind. You may want to have your meetings, make your appointments, finish your business, and jump the next plane home. After a long day of conferences, you may not have the energy to sample the local cuisine. You may want the comfort of a steak—not the challenges and traps of a foreign menu. You may not care whether French fries are French. Here again, a good modern hotel is in order. You can always save the local flavor for a vacation.

In less-developed countries, modern hotels are a must. They may not be authentic, but at least the rooms are clean and the food is safe. In fact, good modern hotels in less developed countries are even shorter on local flavor than they are in Europe. But unless you've got a strong stomach, the local flavor in Upper Volta or Burma may leave you with a bad case of dysentery.

Modern hotels do perform one service everywhere. They make it easier to get a room. Thanks to modern hotels, there's really no such thing as a filled city any longer. This includes Vienna, Salzburg, and Edinburgh during the festivals, Innsbruck in the winter, and Majorca in the summer. There are always a few rooms to be had somewhere.

Of course, money helps. You have to be willing to pay for what's available. A few dollars to the right desk clerk can also do wonders sometimes. Sometimes a pleasant, insistent manner will suffice. If a filled city is your predicament, always try the biggest hotel in town. You can be sure that someone, sometime will be canceling a reservation, leaving early, or arriving late. Just dress well, position yourself at the desk, look plaintive, and wait for an opening.

Small Hotels and Pensions

The place to really discover a country is a small hotel or *pension*. After all, if you're going to Europe, you might as well meet a few Europeans. And you can't do that in a modern hotel filled with other Americans.

In small hotels and *pensions*, your next-door neighbor is probably a European. You may even have to share a bathroom with a European. A little inconvenient, perhaps, but a great way to meet people. The furnishings, the food, the service, the people—none are cut from American cloth. It's not that we're against the American way. We just think you might as well try something different when you're in a different country.

There are other advantages to small hotels and *pensions* aside from the local atmosphere. Cost, for example. Small hotels are significantly cheaper, sometimes as little as half the price of modern luxury hotels. This can make a difference if you're paying your own way. And they're often better located. Because they tend to occupy older houses and buildings, small hotels and *pensions* are often located downtown, within steps of major businesses and key tourist sights.

Small hotels and *pensions* are much more intimate than modern luxury hotels. Because they're smaller, the proprietor can take personal care of you and his other guests. The food may not match the cuisine of elegant hotel restaurants, but it's usually fine home cooking. No rarified French dishes, but no hamburgers either.

To take full advantage of the pleasures and the low cost of small hotels or *pensions*, you need to spend at least a week. So they're probably not the place for short business trips.

In selecting a local hotel, you have to be more careful in some cities than in others. In Scandinavia, you know that almost any hotel or *pension* is comfortable and clean. The Scandinavians are notoriously clean and proper. You may find it boring and unromantic, but it's a bore you'll con come to appreciate.

Many governments try to take the risk out of hotel selection. They rate the quality of all hotels and pensions and require that the rating be displayed outside the building. So the only risk factor is the country. In Germany, a one-star hotel is perfectly acceptable. In Spain, you'd better be willing to rough it. After a few mistakes, you'll be able to rate a country's rating system.

How to Use Guidebooks

Once you've chosen the *kind* of hotel you want, you still have to pick a hotel. We've already suggested several ways to locate one. Obtain the catalogue of castles and country retreats, if that's your style. Or check out the nearest *pension*. If you want a more detailed guide, however, try one of the following.

The best guides are undoubtedly the Michelin Red Guides (New York: Michelin Publications). In contrast to the Michelin Green Guides, which tell you what to do and what to see in a country, the Red Guides tell you where to stay and where to eat. There's a new edition every year, so make sure yours is current.

You should be more skeptical about the timeliness and accuracy of other guides, but you may want to look at either Fodor's guides (New York: David McKay) or *Europe on Ten Dollars a Day* (again, check for the most recent edition). If you're headed west instead of east, try *Myra Waldo's Travel Guide to the Orient and the Pacific* (New York: Macmillan). For the Caribbean, *Fielding's Caribbean, Including Cuba* (New York: Fielding) is best. Like any good guidebook, Fielding's is revised each year.

What to Take

We've already said that people often judge you, rightly or wrongly, on the basis of superficial characteristics: how you dress, how you act. At no time is this more true than when you travel. After all, very few of the people you meet when you travel get a chance to know you well. Most of your encounters are one-time-only affairs. People have little else to base their opinions on except superficial characteristics.

That's why looking and acting your best are crucial to enjoying any trip away from home. Not because the *purpose* of the trip is to impress people (although that might be part of the purpose on a business or job-hunting trip), but because a trip is more enjoyable if the people you meet are friendly and cooperative.

So choose what you take on a trip with special care. Remember, you're carrying all the signs of your style on your back and in your hands.

A Travel Wardrobe

When you travel, take only the clothes you *absolutely* need, nothing more. Carrying a lot of bags is cumbersome, time-consuming, and expensive. You'll spend what seems like half your trip waiting at luggage terminals and looking for porters. In no event should you take more bags than you can carry 50 yards.

For a short business trip, the ideal solution is to fit everything into a single bag you can slide under your seat. This saves your other hand for a briefcase, it saves you time when you arrive at an airport, and it protects you from the vagaries of baggage handling.

Unfortunately, if you're gone for more than a few days, getting everything into one bag may seem impossible at first. But experienced travelers do it regularly—and not just for two- or three-day trips. With practice and planning, you can live for a week or even two out of a single bag. Of course, we're not recommending that you wear the same clothes every day for seven days. But on a business trip, you can usually get by with one suit, changing only the shirts and ties from day to day.

On a prolonged pleasure trip, or a trip where you'll be staying in one place, the one-bag rule can be relaxed. You can afford to be more generous with yourself. But still, the less baggage you take, the easier it will be for you.

When you pack, just ask yourself whether you *really* need an item before you pack it. The following is a good rule of thumb: Pack everything you think you *absolutely* need. Be strict with yourself. When you're finished, remove half of what you just packed. What's left is what you *really* need. This rule is especially helpful if you're an inveterate overpacker.

To give you an idea of what we mean, we've compiled two sample wardrobes: one for a short business trip, one for a short pleasure trip. Your actual wardrobe will have to follow your personal needs, but here are the basics. Optional items are listed in parentheses.

Two-Day Business Trip
1. Two shirts (one formal, one informal)
2. One tie
3. One pair of gray flannel trousers

4.   One light gray sweater
5.   Two pairs socks
6.   Two pairs shorts
7.   (Two undershirts)
8.   (One pair pajamas)
9.   Folding umbrella
10.   Toiletries

It's winter. You're leaving early in the morning and scheduled to return the following evening. Your first day of clothes is on your back: a three-piece blue wool suit, shirt, tie, and winter overcoat. The suit jacket can double as a blazer for informal activities. Your black shoes and a black belt can be worn with both the suit and the blazer, so you needn't pack others. The extra shirts and tie will give you the additional variety you need.

Remember, few people will see you more than once on this trip so you could probably get by with just the tie you're wearing. This limited wardrobe will give you everything you need, plus a little extra room to pack the novel you're reading and a gift or two you pick up on your way home. And best of all, nothing gets crushed in the process.

Incidentally, it's acceptable to relax the rule against polyester when selecting your travel wardrobe. Especially if you travel a lot or for long periods, the advantages of polyester begin to outweigh the esthetic problems. After all, it *is* convenient to have a suit that looks well-pressed for a business meeting even after you've worn it on a cross-country or trans-Atlantic flight. By the same token, it's convenient to have a shirt that you can wash and drip dry in your hotel room.

So for those *rare* times when it can't be avoided, a polyester mix is acceptable in your suits and shirts. But please, under no circumstances buy anything *double*-knit. It's bad enough to buy a suit that feels like hard plastic. It's beyond comprehension to buy one that looks elastic.

Two-Day Pleasure Trip

1.   (One white dress shirt)
2.   (One tie)
3.   One gray sweater
4.   One short-sleeve cotton shirt
5.   One tennis shirt
6.   One pair tennis shorts
7.   One swimsuit
8.   One pair black socks
9.   Two pairs white socks
10.   Two pairs underwear
11.   (Two undershirts)
12.   (One pair pajamas)
13.   One pair tennis shoes
14.   (One folding umbrella)
15.   Toiletries

It's summer and you're wearing a pair of khaki trousers, a blue and white striped shirt, and a blue blazer. That will suffice for an informal evening out. An optional white shirt and tie are included for more formal occasions. This wardrobe may seem skimpy, but it can be pruned even further. The tennis clothes are unnecessary if you don't plan to play tennis. (Of course, if you're a runner, you may want to substitute a set of jogging shoes and shorts.) The folding umbrella may be unnecessary if rain is unlikely.

Luggage

Your luggage, like your wardrobe, should be tailored to the trip you're taking. If you're planning to explore the Amazon in an inflatable raft, a waterproof knapsack might be handy. If you want to spend a week gambling in Monte Carlo, you'll need eight matched pieces of Louis Vuitton luggage—or at least a cheap imitation.

Actually, for most of us, going on a trip doesn't mean challenging the Brazilian jungle in a raft *or* mingling with the jet set at some chic European watering hole. Going on a trip means meeting a client in New York, visiting relatives in California, or seeing London for the first time.

For this kind of travel, we recommend simple, molded plastic luggage in dark colors, preferably dark gray. Look to its price, its strength, its lightness, and the simplicity of its design. Escort luggage by American Tourister may be the best on all counts. It's not fancy, but it's decent looking, cheap, and almost indestructible.

It doesn't really make much sense to buy hand-crafted leather luggage. Most of it looks terrible anyway. Louis Vuitton, for example, leaves not a single rule of style unviolated. It's elaborate to the point of fussiness, it's covered with the designer's logo, and it's indecently expensive. If you're striving for style, it would be less fatal to wear Gucci shoes and carry a lap dog.

But we want to discourage expensive luggage no matter how good it looks. And there is *some* that looks very good indeed. In fact, a fine hand-crafted Florentine leather suitcase isn't just good looking; it's a work of art. But the beauty is ephemeral. Put it in a display case and you can admire it. Put it on a conveyer belt and you can say goodbye.

The problem is that the men behind the belt who handle all that luggage are immune to the pleasures (and fragility) of good leather, hand-stitching, and classic design. After a single trip, your sturdy plastic American Tourister will emerge from the luggage compartment almost unscathed. Your elegant Florentine leather will be scratched and scarred beyond repair.

But baggage handlers are only half the problem. Thieves are the other half. They're *not* immune to the pleasures (and implications) of a richly appointed suitcase. When you're in doubt about what's stylish, common sense is a good substitute.

For More Information

Thomas Graves, *The Rich Man's Guide to Europe* (New York: Prentice-Hall, 1969).

Bill Muster, *Rand McNally's Traveler's Almanac/International Guide* (New York: Rand McNally, 1975).

Pan Am's World Guide: The Encyclopedia of Travel (New York: McGraw-Hill, 1976).